Disinformation in Mass Media

The founding in 1777 of the *Journal de Paris*, France's first daily and distinctly commercial paper, represents an early use of disinformation as a tool for political gain, profit, and societal division. To attract a large readership and bar competition for C.W. Gluck's works at the Paris Opéra, it launched a prolonged campaign of anonymous lies, mockery, and defamation against two prominent members of the Académie Française who wished the Opéra to be open to all deserving composers but lacked a comparable daily forum with which to defend themselves. In this unique episode, music served as a smokescreen for nefarious activity. No musical knowledge is necessary to follow this purely political drama.

Beverly Jerold is a writer and practising musician based in New Jersey, USA.

Royal Musical Association Monographs
Series Editor: Simon P. Keefe

This series was originally supported by funds made available to the Royal Musical Association from the estate of Thurston Dart, former King Edward Professor of Music at the University of London. The editorial board is the Publications Committee of the Association.

No. 32: *Upper-Voice Structures and Compositional Process in the Ars Nova Motet*
Anna Zayaruznaya

No. 33: *The Cyclic Mass: Anglo-Continental Exchange in the Fifteenth Century*
James Cook

No. 34: *The Pre-History of The Midsummer Marriage: Narratives and Speculations*
Roger Savage

No. 35: *Felice Giardini and Professional Music Culture in mid-eighteenth-century London*
Cheryll Duncan

No. 36: *Disinformation in Mass Media: Gluck, Piccinni, and the Journal de Paris*
Beverly Jerold

For more information about this series, please visit: www.routledge.com/music/series/RMA

Disinformation in Mass Media
Gluck, Piccinni, and the *Journal de Paris*

Beverly Jerold

LONDON AND NEW YORK

First published 2021
by Routledge
2 Park Square, Milton Park, Abingdon, Oxon OX14 4RN

and by Routledge
52 Vanderbilt Avenue, New York, NY 10017

Routledge is an imprint of the Taylor & Francis Group, an informa business

© 2021 Beverly Jerold

The right of Beverly Jerold to be identified as author of this work has been asserted by her in accordance with sections 77 and 78 of the Copyright, Designs and Patents Act 1988.

All rights reserved. No part of this book may be reprinted or reproduced or utilised in any form or by any electronic, mechanical, or other means, now known or hereafter invented, including photocopying and recording, or in any information storage or retrieval system, without permission in writing from the publishers.

Trademark notice: Product or corporate names may be trademarks or registered trademarks, and are used only for identification and explanation without intent to infringe.

British Library Cataloguing-in-Publication Data
A catalogue record for this book is available from the British Library

Library of Congress Cataloging-in-Publication Data
A catalog record has been requested for this book

ISBN: 978-0-367-35017-8 (hbk)
ISBN: 978-0-429-32931-9 (ebk)

Typeset in Times New Roman
by Deanta Global Publishing Services, Chennai, India

Contents

	References	vi
	Introduction	1
1	The cast and setting	3
2	Arnaud's correspondence to Italy	24
3	The *Journal de Paris* on the offensive	37
4	Libel of La Harpe by allusion	62
5	The *Armide* episode	79
6	Piccinni's opera and further events	91
7	Disinterested observers	109
8	Profit and power	118
	Timeline of major events	129
	Index	132

References

Journals

AL	*L'Année litteraire* (Paris and Amsterdam, 1754–1791).
CPL	*Courier politique et littéraire* (London, 1777–1778).
JL	*Journal de littérature, des sciences & des arts* (Paris, 1779–1783).
JP	*Journal de Paris* (Paris, 1 January 1777–5 October 1792).
JPL	*Journal de politique et de littérature* (Paris, 1774–1778).
MF	*Mercure de France* (Paris, 1760–1810).
MM	*Magazin der Musik* (Hamburg, 1783–1786).

General

Angermüller	Rudolph Angermüller, 'Alexander Beloselsky "De la musique en Italie"', *Mitteilungen der Internationalen Stiftung Mozarteum* 49/3–4 (2001): 5–52.
Arnaud	François Arnaud, *La soirée perdue à l'opéra* (Avignon, 1776).
Arnold	R.J. Arnold, *Grétry's Operas and the French Public: From the Old Regime to the Restoration* (Farnham: Ashgate, 2016).
Asow	Hedwig and E.H. Mueller von Asow, *The Collected Correspondence and Papers of Christoph Willibald Gluck* (London: Barrie and Rockliff, 1962).
Berlioz-1	Hector Berlioz, *A Travers Chants*, ed. Léon Guichard (Paris: Gründ, 1971).
Berlioz-2	———, *The Art of Music and Other Essays (A Travers Chants)*, trans. Elizabeth Csicsery-Ronay (Bloomington: Indiana University Press, 1994).

References vii

Berlioz-3	Hector Berlioz, *La critique musicale 1823–1863*, ed. H. Robert Cohen and Yves Gérard, 7 vols. (Paris: Editions Buchet/Chastel, c. 1996–).
Braunbehrens	Volkmar Braunbehrens, *Maligned Master. The Real Story of Antonio Salieri*, trans. E.L. Kanes (New York: Fromm, 1992).
Burney-1	Charles Burney, *An Eighteenth-Century Musical Tour in France and Italy*, ed. Percy A. Scholes (London: Oxford, 1959).
Burney-2	———, *A General History of Music* (1789), ed. Frank Mercer, 2 vols. (New York, 1935).
Charlton	David Charlton, *Opera in the Age of Rousseau* (Cambridge: Cambridge University Press, 2012).
CL	*Correspondance littéraire, philosophique et critique par Grimm, Diderot, Raynal, Meister, etc.*, ed. Maurice Tourneux, 16 vols. (Paris: Garnier, 1877–1882).
Coquéau	Claude-Philbert Coquéau, *Entretiens sur l'état actuel de l'Opéra de Paris* (Amsterdam, Paris, 1779).
CS	[Métra, Imbert de Boudeaux, Grimod de la Reynière, etc.], *Correspondance secrète, politique et littéraire, ou Mémoires pour servir à l'histoire des cours, des sociétés & de la littérature en France, depuis la mort de Louis XV*, 18 vols. (London: John Adamson, 1787–1790).
Darlow	Mark Darlow, *Dissonance in the Republic of Letters: The Querelle des Gluckistes et des Piccinnistes* (London: Legenda, 2013).
Darnton	Robert Darnton, *The Literary Underground of the Old Regime* (Cambridge: Harvard University Press, 1982).
Desnoires	Gustave Desnoiresterres, *La Musique française au XVIIIe siècle: Gluck et Piccinni, 1774–1800*, 2nd edn. (Paris: Didier, 1875).
Diderot	Denis Diderot, *Oeuvres complètes de Denis Diderot*, 20 vols., ed. J. Assézat (Paris: Garnier, 1875).
DJ	*Dictionnaire des journaux 1600–1789*, ed. Jean Sgard (Paris: Universitas, 1991).
Du Barry	Jeanne Bécu Du Barry, *Mémoires de Madame la comtesse Du Barri* (Paris: Marne et Delaunay-Vallée, 1829–1830).

EMM	*Encyclopédie méthodique. Musique*, ed. N. Framery and P.-L. Ginguené (Paris: Panckoucke, 1791).
Escherny	François-Louis d'Escherny, *Mélanges de littérature, d'histoire, de morale et de philosophie*, 2 vols. (Paris: Bossange & Masson, 1811).
Fétis	François-Joseph Fétis, *Biographie universelle des musiciens*, 8 vols. (Bruxelles: Leroux, 1835–1844).
Forkel	Johann Nicolaus Forkel, *Musikalischer Almanach für Deutschland auf das Jahr 1789* (Leipzig, 1789).
Galiani	*L'abbé F. Galiani correspondance avec Madame D'Epinay*, ed. L. Percy and G. Maugras, 2nd edn. (Paris: C. Lévy, 1881).
Garat	Dominique-Joseph Garat, *Mémoires historiques sur le XVIIIe siècle, et sur M. Suard* (Paris: Belin, 1821).
Geoffroy	Julien-Louis Geoffroy, *Cours de littérature dramatique*, 2nd edn., 6 vols. (Paris: P. Blanchard, 1825).
Ginguené	Pierre-Louis Ginguené, *Notice sur la vie et les ouvrages de Nicolas Piccinni* (Paris: Panckoucke, An IX [1800 or1801]).
Howard	Patricia Howard, *Gluck. An Eighteenth-Century Portrait in Letters and Documents* (Oxford: Clarendon, 1995).
Isherwood	Robert M. Isherwood, 'The Third War of the Musical Enlightenment', in *Studies in Eighteenth-Century Culture*, ed. Harold Pagliaro (Madison: University of Wisconsin Press, 1975), 4:223–45.
Jerold-1	Beverly Jerold, *Music Performance Issues: 1600–1900* (Hillsdale: Pendragon, 2016).
Jerold-2	———, 'Diderot (Part I)—Authorship and Illusion', *Music Theory & Analysis* 1/1&2 (2014): 38–60.
Jerold-3	———, *The Complexities of Early Instrumentation: Winds and Brass* (Turnhout: Brepols, 2015).
Kaplan	James M. Kaplan, 'Marmontel et Polymnie', vol. 229 in *Studies on Voltaire and the Eighteenth Century* (Oxford: Voltaire Foundation at the Taylor Institution, 1984).
Laborde	Jean-Benjamin de Laborde, *Essai sur la musique ancienne et moderne*, 4 vols. (Paris, 1780).
La Harpe-1	Jean-François de La Harpe, *Correspondance littéraire adressée à son altesse impériale Mgr le Grand-Duc*

	aujourd'hui Empereur de Russie ..., 2nd edn., 6 vols. (Paris: Migneret, an IX. 1801–1807).
La Harpe-2	———, *Correspondance inédite de Jean-François de La Harpe*, ed. Alexandre Jovicevich (Paris: Éditions Universitaires, 1965).
[Leblond]	Anonymous, but attributed to Gaspar Michel Leblond by F.-J. Fétis (1840), who wrote that Abbé Leblond, 'united in bonds of friendship with Abbé Arnaud', assembled the collection, *Mémoires pour servir à l'histoire de la révolution opérée dans la musique par M. le chevalier Gluck* (Naples, 1781; rpt. 1967 and *QGP*, vol.1). Arnaud probably provided the commentary.
Lettre	Anonymous, *Lettre à Monsieur de La Harpe, ou Observations critiques sur son Journal; Par DAVID *** son ami* (London, 1777). https://gallica.bnf.fr
Mannlich	Johann Christian von Mannlich, 'Mémoires sur la musique à Paris à la fin du règne de Louis XV', ed. H. von Trostprugg, *La Revue musicale* 15 (1934): 111–262.
Marmontel-1	Jean-François Marmontel, *Essai sur les révolutions de la musique, en France* [Paris, 1777]. https://book.google.com.
Marmontel-2	———, *Mémoires*, ed. John Renwick (Clermont-Ferrand: G. de Bussac, 1972).
Marmontel-3	———, *Memoirs of Marmontel*, translator unspecified (London: H.S. Nichols, 1895).
Marmontel-4	———, *Correspondance*, ed. John Renwick, 2 vols. (Clermont-Ferrand: G. de Bussac, 1974).
Martini-1	Giovanni Battista Martini, *Padre Martini's Collection of Letters*, an index by Anne Schnoebelen (New York: Pendragon, 1979).
Martini-2	———, *Storia della musica*, 2 vols. (Bologna, 1770).
Mossner	Ernest Campbell Mossner, *The Life of David Hume*, 2nd edn. (Oxford: Clarendon, 1980).
Mozart	*Mozart Briefe und Aufzeichnungen*, ed. W.A. Bauer and O.E. Deutsch, 7 vols. (Kassel: Bärenreiter, 1962–1975).
MS	[Louis Petit de Bachaumont, *et al.*], *Mémoires secrets pour servir à l'histoire de la république des lettres en France*, 36 vols. (London: John Adamson, 1780–1789).

NG	*The New Grove Dictionary of Music and Musicians*, ed. S. Sadie and J. Tyrrell, 2nd edn., 29 vols. (London: Macmillan, 2001).
Pipers	*Pipers Enzyklopädie des Musiktheatres*, ed. Carl Dahlhaus, 6 vols. (München, Zurich: Piper, 1991).
Pougin	Arthur Pougin, *Pierre Jélyotte et les chanteurs de son temps* (Paris, 1905).
QGP	*Querelle des Gluckistes et des Piccinnistes: Texte des pamphlets avec introduction, commentaire et index, par François Lesure*, 2 vols. (Geneva: Minkoff, 1984).
Rasmussen	Dennis C. Rasmussen, *The Infidel and the Professor. David Hume, Adam Smith, and the Friendship That Shaped Modern Thought* (Princeton and Oxford: Princeton University Press, 2017).
Reichardt	Anon, Bruchstücke aus Reichardt's *'Autobiographie'*, *Allgemeine musikalische Zeitung* 15 (Leipzig, 13 October 1813), 665–74.
Ricci	Corrado Ricci, *I teatri di Bologna nei secoli XVII e XVIII: storia aneddotica* (Bologna: Monti, 1888; rpt. 1965).
Rousseau	Jean-Jacques Rousseau, *Collection complète des oeuvres* (Geneva, 1780–1789): https://rousseauonline.ch; 17 vols. with Supplements.
Schmid	Anton Schmid, *Christoph Willibald Ritter von Gluck* (Leipzig: Fr. Fleischer, 1854).
Vatielli	Francesco Vatielli, 'Riflessi della lotta Gluckista in Italia', *Rivista musicale italiana* 21 (1914): 639–71.
Vauthier	G. Vauthier, 'L'École royale de chant', Part IV. (1784–1791), *La Revue musicale* 11/12 (1911–1912): 294–99.
Voltaire	Voltaire, *Correspondance*, ed. Theodore Besterman, 13 vols. (Paris, c. 1977–c. 1993).
Zaretsky	Robert Zaretsky and John T. Scott, *The Philosophers' Quarrel: Rousseau, Hume, and the Limits of Human Understanding* (New Haven: Yale University Press, 2009).

Introduction

> Truth exists, only falsehood has to be invented.
> —Georges Braque (*Pensées sur l'Art*)

Modern literature has documented many eighteenth-century French literary quarrels on subjects of every description, but the one concerning the operas of Christoph Willibald Gluck (1714–1787) and Niccolò Piccinni (1728–1800) is worthy of re-examination because it represents an early instance of using daily mass media to sow discord in society at large for political advantage. Before the advent of journalism as a commercial business, eighteenth-century journals and papers were modest enterprises that appeared at varying intervals with content for the educated elite. This form of journalism underwent an abrupt change in 1777 with the founding of the *Journal de Paris* (*JP*), a daily paper directed to a large audience in a metropolitan area. Like today, mass media confers great benefits, but can also be used for nefarious purposes. Modern opinion about this *querelle*, drawn principally from material in the *JP* reprinted in a 1781 volume, is generally critical of Piccinni's supporters:

> Marmontel wrote the most abrasive of Piccinnist pamphlets, *Essai sur les révolutions de la musique en France*, in which he compared the melodic truth of the periodic style established by Vinci with the alleged barbarity of Gluck ... In [his memoirs], he gave a full, if naturally biased, account of his theatrical career and his collaborations with composers.
> A dogmatic critic with little understanding of music, he [Jean-François de La Harpe] joined with Marmontel to support the Italians against Gluck, and particularly favoured Sacchini; his virulent attack on *Armide* in the *Journal de politique et de littérature* (5 October 1777) was ridiculed by Gluck himself in the *Journal de Paris* (12 October 1777) and by La Harpe's colleague J. B. A. Suard using the pseudonym 'L'anonyme de Vaugirard.'[1]

We would thus take the quarrel to be a musical one, but the truth lies elsewhere. No knowledge of music is necessary to follow this purely political drama in which music was only a pretext for defamatory anonymous attacks on individuals of sound reputation to ensure both the success of the new *JP* and Gluck's continued domination at the Paris Opéra—with all its glory, fame, and wealth. Ruthless power unleashed by a new medium for financial gain is the subject. Here, disinformation on a grand scale was born. By publishing on a daily basis to a large readership, its influence far exceeded anything that literary and political journals could offer in response. This aspect of the quarrel sets it apart from earlier ones.

Judging from Mark Darlow's extensive bibliography in *Dissonance in the Republic of Letters: The Querelle des Gluckistes et des Piccinnistes*,[2] this matter has generated substantial interest today. For the period before 1777, he offers detailed accounts of the century's musical quarrels, differences in aesthetic views, political context, opera reform, and so on. Especially useful is his Catalogue of Quarrel Texts in the Appendix, which includes 128 items from 1772 to 1783. For the period from 1772 through 1776, nearly all of the 23 cited texts are either in praise of Gluck or on his behalf, so there was no quarrel during this period, but merely the usual difference of opinion. With the founding of the *JP* in January 1777, the number of texts skyrocketed to 78 for this year alone, with 55 appearing in the *JP*, nearly all anonymous. The present book will add still more sources.

According to Darlow and other modern writers, the quarrel concerned 'the seemingly trivial question of whether Gluck's reform made him a worthy messiah of the future of French lyric theatre or whether the Neapolitan Niccolò Piccinni should be preferred'.[3] *Au contraire*, it concerned tolerance of differing views and opening the Paris Opéra to any deserving composer. In his conclusion, Darlow is correct on a number of points; for example, the controversy was unrelated to earlier disputes over French vs. Italian music and was not just tolerated by the authorities, but explicitly encouraged by the crown. When treating the quarrel itself, however, he (like earlier authors) wrote without knowledge of the events traced in this book, which then affected interpretation. These events explain the vehement discord set in motion by this most unusual episode.

Notes

1 *NG*, 'Marmontel' and 'La Harpe', respectively.
2 Darlow.
3 Ibid, 1.

1 The cast and setting

To set the stage for the following account, this chapter supplies essential background material about the *Journal de Paris* (*JP*), the major figures in the controversy, and the events prior to the quarrel. Informed criticism from the period indicates that the level of performance bore no resemblance to our own. Astonishing volume and high-pitched emotion were what drew a crowd in Paris, appalling those of a greater sensibility. Although Christoph Willibald Gluck improved performance standards, he was advised to retain these elements. Knowledge of this factor is vital to understanding the criticism that followed. As Wolfgang Amadeus Mozart's letter of 9 July 1778, written from Paris to his father, observed, French singers 'really should not be called such—for they do not sing, but scream—howl—that is, from the whole neck, from the nose and throat'.[1]

A new print medium

A daily metropolitan newspaper with a monopoly held enormous power to distort facts, ridicule individuals, and publish anything to further its own aims. Such was the case when the first French daily, the *JP*, was founded in January 1777 by Guillaume Olivier de Corancez and three other financiers. Previously, there had been only literary and political journals for the educated elite. In contrast, the *JP* was a commercial enterprise that sought a much larger audience. It aimed low—and then lower. After publishing indiscreet material, it was shut down by the moral censor on 23 January but was permitted to resume publication on the 29th. M. de La Place held the title of director during these first three weeks, but no evidence of a subsequent director is found until 1785.[2]

Resuming publication, the *JP* avoided the censor by exciting controversy through cleverly designed attacks on prominent individuals. The subject used to foment discord was opera—specifically, the German music of Gluck and the Italian music of Niccolò Piccinni. Because most literate

4   *The cast and setting*

people attended the opera for one reason or another, the *JP*'s insulting articles, letters, and epigrams were of intense interest—not for musical reasons, but for the individuals ridiculed, who were members of the select Académie Française. From 1774 through 1777, Gluck's works held a near-monopoly at the Académie Royale de Musique (the formal name for the Paris Opéra), but what has been called the 'Quarrel of the Gluckists and Piccinnists' did not erupt until shortly after the *JP*, which had strong Gluckist affiliations, was founded. In 1773, negotiations had begun with Piccinni about composing for the Opéra, but after his arrival in Paris (just before 1777), the Gluckists maintained that Italian music was suitable only in concerts and at the Comédie-Italienne (where it posed no competition). Those who supported Piccinni's right to be heard simply wanted deserving talent to have access to the Opéra. Despite citing Gluck's strong points, they faced a barrage of anonymous humiliation, lies, and defamation in the *JP*, with little to defend themselves. Although history has assumed that the matter concerned musical issues, in reality, it was political. The texts and events reveal manipulation of public opinion on a grand scale and substantial financial rewards for the new paper and its supporters.

Although the controversy continued for several years, most of the literary action took place in 1777. Scholars such as James M. Kaplan have puzzled over the high passions aroused: 'What is perhaps most intriguing to posterity is the violent bitterness of this quarrel. One is astonished ... that a question of music was able to arouse such sharp emotions.'[3] Some salient facts that do much to explain the curious events of 1777 have lain hidden.

The major figures

For the Gluckists, who always published anonymously, the protagonists were later revealed to be the Abbé François Arnaud (1721–1784), a Greek scholar, and Jean-Baptiste-Antoine Suard (1734–1817), a specialist in English studies who wrote under the pseudonym *L'Anonyme de Vaugirard*. From 1762 to 1771, they had co-edited the monarchy's approved *Gazette de France*. The librettist for Gluck's first Paris opera, François-Louis Le Bland Du Roullet (1716–1786), formerly an attaché at the French embassy in Vienna, probably wrote the letters signed by Gluck and perhaps others.

Those who supported Piccinni's right to be heard wrote only in response to repeated attacks from the Gluckists but quickly ceased in order to avoid further attacks. In 1777, nearly all of their known writings appeared in the *Journal de politique et de littérature* (*JPL*), edited by Jean-François de La Harpe (1739–1803), and a scholarly *Essai sur les révolutions de la musique, en France* by Jean-François Marmontel (1723–1799), librettist for Piccinni's first Paris opera. As the author of influential works such as the

Contes moraux, Bélisaire, and *Les Incas, ou Le Destruction de l'empire du Pérou,* as well as plays and articles for the *Encyclopédie, ou Dictionnaire raisonné,* Marmontel had the greatest literary reputation among these writers. His opposition to the class structure of the day and advocacy of equal opportunity marked him as a man ahead of his time and did not endear him to the aristocracy. When the English music historian Charles Burney visited Paris in 1770, he met these writers and was invited to a dinner gathering at Suard's, where La Harpe 'seems the youngest of these literary gentlemen, and the Fag for them all' (in English public-school parlance, a junior who performs certain duties for a senior).[4] Of these five writers, only Du Roullet was not a member of the Académie Française.

In contrast to the Gluckists' voluminous anonymous writing, the source for the scanty Piccinnist material could be easily identified. Marmontel's *Essai* includes much neutral material about French opera and La Harpe's journal contains balanced reviews of Gluck's operas, two responses to the *L'Anonyme de Vaugirard's* distortion of these reviews, and a reply to one of Gluck's letters.

This episode reflected the two wings at the Académie Française. In 1771, Friedrich Melchior von Grimm's *Correspondance littéraire* (*CL*), which circulated only to foreign courts, had observed that its members were divided into two opposing factions:

> the *dévot* [religious] party, which combines with the prelates all the academicians of slight merit, who consequently are especially zealous to make their case with baseness; and the *philosophique* party, which the *dévots* call encyclopedic, and which comprises all men of letters who think with a bit of loftiness and daring, and who prefer independence and a limited fortune to the favours obtained only by grovelling and lying.[5]

Not all with religious affiliation were members of the *dévot* party, for some had more liberal views. When Suard was admitted to the Académie in 1774, the *CL* reported that his initial discourse had not produced the effect for which his friends had hoped. They had been obliged to acknowledge that he had not displayed all his strengths, and his opponents had remarked that 'he had contented himself with proving to us at great length that he was a good Christian, which was not at all what was important to prove to the Académie'.[6] Thus the Gluckists belonged to the Académie's *dévot* wing, while the Piccinnists were *philosophes*. 'An ill wind blowing on philosophy' is what Voltaire called the years of this quarrel, which saw an awakening of reactionary forces in France. The *dévots*, who had overthrown Anne-Robert-Jacques Turgot (economist, politician, and friend of the *philosophes*), acclaimed Gluck's operas to a remarkable degree.[7]

6 *The cast and setting*

Figure 1.1 Portrait of Jean-François Marmontel from his *Contes moraux* (1765).

Writing to La Harpe on 6 October 1777, Voltaire praised his journal, calling it the only one he read: 'You are, in my opinion, the legislator of taste and reason ... We greatly need you to avoid becoming barbarians subsisting solely on Italian and German music.' He also thanked Marmontel for honouring him with the lyre's sweetest sounds.[8] In his letter to Voltaire (18 November 1777), Jean Le Rond d'Alembert mentioned that the musical

Figure 1.2 Portrait of Jean-François de La Harpe. Houghton Library, Harvard University.

controversy had begun again between La Harpe and Suard/Arnaud. He believed La Harpe to be completely justified, but observed that it 'has led to much acrimony among us ... All that will be nothing, my dear colleague, if you support philosophy and your friends'.[9]

The 1781 reprint of Gluckist texts

Modern scholars have utilized texts reprinted in the 491-page *Mémoires pour servir à l'histoire de la révolution opérée dans la musique par M. le chevalier Gluck* ('Leblond' collection, 1781), attributed to Abbé Gaspard Michel Leblond, an archaeologist who collaborated with Arnaud in numismatic studies.[10] The *Journal de littérature, des sciences & des arts* (*JL*) (1781) found it to be almost entirely a Gluckist document.[11] Verifiable Piccinnist writing comprises (1) out-of-context quotations from La Harpe's

Figure 1.3 Portrait of François Arnaud. Bibliothèque natonale de France.

journal with Suard's anonymous critique and (2) Marmontel's *Essai* with the editor's copious critical footnotes. The peremptory preface of this collection presages its contents:

> Everyone agrees that to judge painting it is not enough to have eyes. But many people claim that it is enough to have ears to judge music. From that stem these ardent debates, these eternal disputes about the sweetest and most pleasing of the arts.
> When M. le Chevalier Gluck brought us his *Iphigénie en Aulide* in 1774, the public and some first-rank men of letters were divided over its merit. The public, which does not regulate its pleasures according to some opinions and phrases, seems to agree today in favour of the composer of *Orphée, Alceste, Armide* and the two *Iphigénies*, but the men

Figure 1.4 Portrait of Jean-Baptiste-Antoine Suard. Musée de la Révolution française.

of letters, of whom a very large number consider their opinions much more than their pleasures, still argue with a type of obstinacy—some for the art's interests; others, out of conceit.

Long before M. Gluck came to France, the most perceptive and enlightened connoisseurs of Italy had proposed him as a model to all the dramatic composers of their country … This agreement among the principal connoisseurs of the different nations of Europe would doubtless suffice to gain the approbation of a deaf person, but all the ages have taught us how difficult it is to tear the solemn confession of error from people who believe themselves destined to create and direct public opinion.

Moreover, since the revolution in theatre music made by M. le Chevalier Gluck is one of the most important and most brilliant epochs in the history of this beautiful art, an unassuming music lover has dedicated himself to assembling the diverse writings that have appeared on this subject, for and against. The French are always stimulated to emulate the Athenians. Doubtless, it would be necessary to exclude those of our fashionable people and men of letters who would attach some glory to scorning the discussions in which the Athenians took so much interest.[12]

This preface, with its exaggeration of facts (as Gluck's lack of popularity in Italy will be shown), can be attributed to Arnaud, who tends to remind the reader that he is an authority on ancient Greece. Contrary to what this quotation implies, no one of reputation was opposed to Gluck. The Piccinnists sought only that the Opéra be open to all composers of talent.

Like other Gluckist material, the 'Leblond' collection was published anonymously. Most of it appeared originally in the *JP* as attacks on Marmontel and La Harpe in support of Gluck—approximately 40 of the 52 items from 1777 and all but one of those from 1778. Other pieces praising Gluck were published mainly as pamphlets. The collection omits the *JP*'s more virulent material. Although A.E. Barbier's *Dictionnaire des ouvrages anonymes* (1872–1879) lists only the contributors to this volume,[13] François-Joseph Fétis (1840) said that Leblond, 'united in bonds of friendship with Abbé Arnaud', assembled the collection. Leblond may have done the chores for publication, but the preface bears Arnaud's stamp. He probably also chose the selections and wrote the critical commentary about Marmontel's *Essai*, as well as the other editorial additions. According to Fétis, Leblond had no literary works beyond this compilation.[14] Therefore, Arnaud is the more plausible editor.

In 1984 François Lesure published a reprint of further writings, including some that support the Piccinnist cause. It errs, however, in attributing to them the anonymous *Problême qui occupe la capitale de la monarchie française; on demande si Mr. Glouck est plus grand musicien que Mr. Piccini* (1777), whose 22 small pages leap from one topic to another, from a bit of French history to a view on ladies' fashions.[15] The small music portion has the same tone as the fabricated letter of 6 July 1779 purported to be from 'Les Piccinnists' (see Chapter 6), and the last page accuses Gluck of plagiarizing several composers. The tract probably originated with the Gluckist camp to sow discord.

Today's general conviction that the Gluckists were right seems to parallel nineteenth-century views, as summarized by Friedrich Nietzsche:

> Unfortunately in the aesthetic wars, which artists provoke by their works and apologias for their works, just as is the case in real war, it is might and not reason that decides. All the world now assumes as a historical fact that, in his dispute with Piccini, Gluck was in the right. At any rate, he was victorious, and had might on his side.[16]

Gluck indeed had might on his side, much of which was concentrated in the *JP*.

Journalism at the new paper

Although Gluck spent a considerable amount of time in Paris between 1774 and 1776 preparing his operas *Iphigénie en Aulide*, *Orphée*, *Cythère assiégée*, and *Alceste*, there was no significant dispute until the *JP* began its series of attacks shortly after beginning publication. Suard, closely associated with the *JP* in its early stages, was later named its *censeur*.

Nothing sells papers like controversy. The *JP* took an unusually strong position in favour of Gluck when vilifying La Harpe and Marmontel. No matter how many favourable things they said about Gluck's work, the slightest criticism served as a pretext for launching against them a varied assortment of long unsigned sarcastic articles, anonymous letters of ridicule, and insulting epigrams. Piccinni did not arrive in Paris until the end of December 1776, and his first opera was not staged until January 1778, by which time this particular episode was over. There was good reason for not criticizing Piccinni himself or his music in print. With Marie Antoinette's sister reigning as Queen of the Two Sicilies, which included Naples, any criticism of Piccinni could have cost the Gluckists the young French queen's support (Gluck had been her teacher in Vienna). Instead, they concentrated their attacks on those who supported Piccinni. In essence, the music issues were nothing but a smokescreen for personal attacks on individuals. This explains why emotions ran so high.

By presenting themselves as opposed to the introduction of any Italian music at the Paris Opéra and maintaining that it belonged only in concerts, the Gluckists were viewed as intolerant. In the 'Leblond' reprint of Marmontel's *Essai*, the editor comments: 'This [Italian] melody could also be the delight of Chevalier Gluck's partisans, but only in concerts, and not in the theatre where it offends against all conventions.'[17]

The activities of Gluck's associate

Gluck's letters indicate a close relationship with his librettist Du Roullet, whose ties in both Vienna and Paris facilitated the composer's entry at the Opéra. He seems to have functioned also as a business manager, handling administrative details on behalf of Gluck. Yet some of his actions were questionable at best. To ensure the success of his and Gluck's *Iphigénie en Aulide* (1774), Du Roullet is said to have put a coterie of his friends at the head of a cabal. This is also suggested by a stanza from a satiric chanson published in both the *CL* and the *Mémoires secrets* (*MS*) (January 1776), in which he is portrayed as giving orders (Le Bailli is the title associated with his membership in the Knights of Malta):

– Toi, chef de mes athlètes,	– You, chief of my athletes,
Qui dans ce pays-ci	Who in this country
Sais mesurer les têtes,	Knows how to contend,
Sois mon superbe appui;	Be my superb support;
Cours, cabale au parterre;	Cours, cabal on the *parterre*;[18]
Du fond je t'ai saisi,	I have given you the groundwork,
La forme est ton affaire.	The form is your affair.
– Oui, monsieur Le Bailli.[19]	– Yes, M. Le Bailli.

Among Du Roullet's various schemes is one of particular interest. In 1782, he persuaded the Opéra to mount *Les Danaïdes*, presented to the committee as entirely by Gluck, but subsequently amended to be two-thirds by Gluck, who dictated the remainder to Antonio Salieri (certified by Du Roullet and Salieri in official documents). When the opera's success was assured some three weeks after it opened, Du Roullet produced a letter from Gluck affirming that the music was entirely Salieri's.[20] According to the German journalist Carl Friedrich Cramer, this had been planned well in advance with Gluck's participation.[21] The Opéra's policy is conveyed in a document of 27 February 1778: 'An author convicted of having submitted his work under the name of another to procure an entry for himself will immediately be deprived of his rights forever.'[22] Neither Gluck nor Salieri received any penalty.

On 4 August 1786, the *MS* reported that Du Roullet had died: 'He was a man of great wit, but a mediocre author.' According to the *MS*, his chief accomplishment was making Chevalier Gluck known in France and writing the libretto for his *Iphigénie en Aulide*. Otherwise, he was a *petit-maître* (fop), an *agréable* with a long record of *fatuité*.[23]

Events before 1777

The roots of the controversy extend back several years. To ameliorate the Opéra's financial problems, the Neapolitan ambassador Domenico Carraccioli advocated importing a composer celebrated in one of the great centres of Italian opera. Piccinni was mentioned as having the suitable qualities. Jean-Benjamin de Laborde (author of the *Essai sur la musique ancienne et moderne*, 1780) was engaged to open negotiations with him in Naples; the official document for the three-month journey is dated 19 June 1773.[24] In a letter of 4 September 1773 to the writer Louise d'Epinay in Paris, the Italian economist Ferdinando Galiani reported that Laborde was in Naples.[25] Her letter of 25 April 1774 to Galiani described the premiere of Gluck's *Iphigénie en Aulide*, adding: 'As usual [at the Opéra], it was all screamed instead of sung. They say that Piccinni is leaving you to come here. I do not believe a word of it and will wait for your confirmation.'[26] Thus, a rumour was circulating that Piccinni's arrival was imminent, but the king's death on 10 May 1774 interrupted the production of *Iphigénie* in the middle of its run for a period of mourning. According to Piccinni's biographer Pierre-Louis Ginguené (1748–1816), Laborde's negotiations with Piccinni were nearly complete when the king died. As soon as the new court was able to deal with such matters, the Neapolitan ambassador obtained the queen's permission to reopen negotiations.[27] This, no doubt, delayed arrangements for bringing Piccinni to Paris. Finally, Galiani's letter of 2 November 1776 informed d'Epinay that she would be seeing Piccinni (whom he recommended highly also to the Baron d'Holbach and others as a *très honnête* man) and his family in 15 days.[28]

Turning to the events that brought Gluck to Paris, we find Du Roullet writing from Vienna on 1 August 1772 to the director of the Opéra (published in the *Mercure de France*, October 1772), offering an opera on which he and Gluck had collaborated.[29] After asserting that Gluck finds the French language superior to the Italian for music, Du Roullet includes a veiled reference to Jean-Jacques Rousseau, who, in 1753, had used strong language to declare the French language unsuitable for music:

> M. Glouch was indignant at rash assertions by those of our famous writers [Rousseau] who have dared to calumniate the French language by maintaining that it did not lend itself to great musical creation.[30]

This was followed by a February 1773 letter in the *Mercure* on the same subject but signed by Gluck (probably written by Du Roullet). Remarkably, it courted Rousseau's support:

> with the help of the famous M. Rousseau of Geneva, whom I intended to consult about seeking a noble, moving and natural melody with a declamation in keeping with the prosody of each language and the character of each people, we might together succeed in finding the medium I have in mind for producing a type of music suited to all nations and eliminating the absurd distinctions between national forms of music. My study of this great man's works on music ... prove the depth of his knowledge and sureness of taste and have filled me with admiration. I was left with the profound conviction that if he had chosen to devote himself to the application of this art, he would have been able to achieve the prodigious effects that the ancients attributed to music. I am delighted to have an opportunity of paying him publicly this tribute which I believe he deserves.[31]

14   *The cast and setting*

This dramatic change of posture indicates that the strategists believed there was more to be gained from having Rousseau on their side. Perhaps they thought it would be useful to cultivate the friendship of Corancez, who was to publish Rousseau's works (and later the *JP*) and who then arranged Gluck's meeting with Rousseau.

Gluck sent Rousseau a score of *Alceste* for his criticism.[32] According to the *MS* dated 24 April 1774, Gluck was responsible for reconciling Rousseau with the Opéra's directors. After attending two rehearsals of Gluck's *Iphigénie*, Rousseau recanted his former position and admitted that 'good foreign music can be composed for French words'.[33] Gluck's stratagem worked, and Rousseau became his advocate, thereby weakening any possible opposition. In its first year of operation, the *JP* flattered Rousseau (who died in 1778) with at least six major articles.[34]

Gluck may have written to Marie Antoinette, his former pupil. On 14 January 1774, the *MS* reported that she had issued him an open invitation to visit at any time.[35] He arrived in Paris with his *Iphigénie en Aulide* late in 1773.

Carraccioli's negotiations with the Paris authorities likely began long before the official approval on 19 June 1773 to engage Piccinni. Thus, there was no attempt, as claimed today, to bring Piccinni to Paris as competition for Gluck. This misapprehension may derive from an entry in the *Mémoires secrets* dated 3 April 1774, which reported intrigues involving the king's mistress:

> The Countess Du Barry's supporters have advised her that she could not enhance her fame more effectively than by undertaking a visible sponsorship of the arts; they have urged her to take a position as rival to the Dauphine in this respect. As the princess strongly protects Sr Gluck and has supported his coming to France, they have persuaded her [Mme Du Barry] to set up a competitor to Gluck in the person of Sr Piccinni, whom she is to summon from Italy.[36]

But Laborde's mission to engage Piccinni, of which this writer seems unaware, preceded the acceptance of Gluck's opera. It was not the countess who summoned Piccinni, but the Italian ambassador, Laborde, and other interested individuals. At this stage, there was no division into Gluckist or Piccinnist camps, and there would be none until the events of 1777 served as the catalyst. In her *Mémoires*, Du Barry recounted her political motives for backing Piccinni.

> a man of genius, true musician, but little inclined to cabals and above every intrigue. More careful of his work than his reputation, he was

a man for whom it was necessary to do everything. I extolled him as much as I could, I did my best to help him, but, unfortunately, it was necessary to form an alliance with Marmontel whose grave pathos has always inspired me with a certain antipathy. For his part, this author has held a grudge against me for many years and could not pardon my boredom and long yawns during the reading of his work at Mme de la Garde's.[37]

That there was friction between these two is scarcely surprising—as the king's mistress living in inconceivable luxury, she symbolized the worst aspects of a monarchy. Acknowledging that she had not supported Piccinni with as much fervour as the Dauphine had Gluck, she admitted that the latter crushed them, 'less perhaps by merit than by an advantageous position'.

Recitative and *air*

To follow the music discussion, it is useful to know the difference between melody (as in the Italian aria or the French *air*) and recitative, which was also called 'declamation' by writers of the period. Recitative seeks to imitate the natural inflections of speech by using relatively few notes within a narrow range and avoiding rhythmic interest. Whereas a good melody is easily retained by the ear, the notes of recitative are usually lost to memory as soon as performed. The tools for music composition can be acquired through instruction, but the gift for creating melody is largely inborn. What makes a melody appealing is not easily defined, but everyone recognizes a fine one when they hear it, whether in the classical or popular idiom. During this period, Italian opera had won acclaim throughout Europe for the melodic beauty of its arias. On the other hand, audiences ignored the austere, simple recitatives that preceded each aria. In contrast, French opera had traditionally offered only brief passages of melody, so audiences were not trained to expect it. As discussed below, they were more interested in a riveting drama. French librettos were designed to be set to music mainly as recitative (but in a more elaborate form that differed from the simple Italian recitative), which is why French opera tends to sound like a continuous recitative, even though it contains brief *airs*. The arias of Italian opera, on the other hand, require poetry with a measured and regular phrase structure. As Marmontel observed, it is no easy task to convert a traditional French libretto into poetry that is supple and receptive to melody. Beginning with his opera *Orfeo* in Vienna, Gluck followed the French manner of emphasizing declamation over melody. In a letter of 26 April 1774, years before the controversy erupted, Turgot conveyed his impressions:

16 *The cast and setting*

> I have finally seen this opera of Gluck. There are some pieces that have given me the greatest pleasure ... but in general I did not find enough melodic pieces. So many recitatives ... or arias very close to recitative style left me wanting something ... I saw nothing at all of what the Abbé Arnaud's enthusiasm had led him to see.[38]

Gluck's lack of melody was the major criticism made of his composition. A secondary one mentioned by Marmontel concerned the manner in which his operas were performed:

> Much has been said about the force, energy and vigour of the sounds that M. Gluck draws from his orchestra or the lungs of his singers; and it must be acknowledged that never has one roared the trumpets, buzzed the strings, and bellowed the voices as he has done. But who knows if Italian melody and harmony do not, in their simplicity, also have some force, with less effort? All the theatres of Europe have felt the effects of a thousand heartfelt pieces, whose song was not noise. ... Does the French ear or soul have so little sensitivity that it needs these intense commotions to be moved?[39]

Extreme volume, however, was what drew a crowd in Paris, and had also been employed in Jean-Philippe Rameau's operas (as d'Epinay implied above). In its review of the 1769 revival of François-André Danican Philidor's tragic opera *Ernelinde*, the *CL* described a composer's trials at the Opéra when attempting to satisfy expectations:

> this work was neither sung nor played; [for] that was not the way to open the ears of the deaf. This is not to say that the Opéra's singers did not do their best, but that their best is poor, their style of singing intolerable to every ear accustomed to music, and their acting as insipid as their singing is poor. Thanks to the art and soul of Mme Larrivée, Ernelinde's delirium, a sublime scene in music, produced yawning at the theatre ... The connoisseurs might criticize this work for not being quiet enough, but the composer has conformed to the taste of his country. He knows that when the eardrum is not broken by sheer noise, one is not thought to have produced music. This interminable hurly-burly of choruses that are bawled endlessly and an orchestra filled with instruments that never rest is intolerable to a man of taste, but ever since the founding of the bombastic Rameau's empire, they have become the essence of French opera. Philidor hoped to find a happy medium. He wanted to satisfy the lovers of French opera by choruses and noise, but also, by speaking the most sublime language [in the remaining portions], captivate those able

to understand it. In trying to satisfy everyone, he really did not captivate anyone ... If ever they in France succeed in knowing what music is, they will be greatly ashamed by this work's failure.[40]

Gluck's directing skills

Those who supported Piccinni gave Gluck credit for improving performance standards. It was generally agreed that conventional French opera was in serious need of an overhaul. Ginguené's assessment corresponds to that of others: heavy and bulky voices; a cold declamation; discordant and immobile choruses; an unskilled, deafening, and monotonous orchestra; and a public accustomed to vocal screaming devoid of song and rhythm. After attempts at reform by individuals such as Philidor, Pierre-Alexandre Monsigny, André-Ernest-Modeste Grétry, and François-Joseph Gossec, the opera always relapsed into torpor and the glacial convulsions of its ancient psalmody (a term comparing the Opéra's dragging pace to the monotonous chanting of Psalms.) The way out of this morass, according to Ginguené, was shown by Gluck:

> It was he who applied on this inert and heavy mass the torch of Prometheus; who made the singers declaim with simplicity and truth, and, as much as possible, sing in tune and in time; who enlivened the choruses; and who trained the orchestra to follow and support the singers' movements and expression.[41]

Ginguené also credits Gluck with making the French forget forever their 'plainsong' by combining the French scheme of opera with the German school's strong harmony and the Italian forms of recitative and melody.

Many people of taste found Gluck's music superior to Rameau's, which suggests other factors in 1774. Instead of composers leading their works, as in Italy, a *batteur de mesure* (time beater) kept the orchestra and singers together with a wooden rod struck audibly. Even so, rhythm and ensemble were said to be greatly lacking. With his garrulous manner, Gluck seems to have been just the person to bring order out of the chaos. Another factor was the burden of heavy ornamentation in Rameau's music.

Both foreign and Parisian commentators criticized French singers for loud, coarse vocal production and lack of a rhythmic pulse. Although the countertenor Joseph Le Gros had an admirable voice, he was called a clumsy, heavy, and unintelligent singer. Gluck was said to have laboured mightily to give him some nobility and dignity. The women, spoiled by adulation and supported by the greatest lords always alert to take up their disputes, were still less prepared for his fastidious criticisms. They believed they had only to sing their role languishingly.[42]

18 *The cast and setting*

In Paris, most composers seem to have played a relatively passive role in rehearsals, but Gluck participated actively. His sound dramatic instincts and musical leadership undoubtedly contributed to the success his operas achieved. The 15 March 1777 issue of La Harpe's *JPL*, just before the major divisive events erupted, recalls the situation at the Opéra when Gluck arrived to prepare his *Iphigénie en Aulide* in 1774, granting him credit for his achievements with the performers:

> He found an orchestra that saw scarcely anything in music but some Cs and Ds; crotchets and quavers; assortments of mannequins called choruses; and singers of whom some were as inanimate as the music they sang while others tried to rekindle the sad, ponderous psalmody or frigid chansons by sheer strength and lungs. Prometheus shook his torch and the statues came to life. Instruments of the orchestra became sensitive voices producing sounds that could be touching or terrible ... The singers learned that when music is both speech-like and expressive it needs only to be well felt to produce a strong and genuine action ... The effect of this new production was extraordinary. For the first time, a *Tragédie en Musique* was viewed with continuous attention from start to finish, and with ever increasing interest.[43]

According to Ginguené, much was required to instil life into the chorus, which was ranged in two immobile lines along the sides:

> This fortunate revolution was reserved for M. Gluck. He needed not only the creativity necessary to conceive choruses that were more dramatic and active than formerly, but also all the means that nature had given him for executing them. At the rehearsals, you should have seen him running from one end of the theatre to the other, in turn urging, pulling, dragging along by the arm, begging, scolding, cajoling the singers—men and women, who, surprised at seeing themselves led in such a way, went from surprise to docility, from docility to expression, to effects that excited them and communicated a part of the composer's soul—you would have had to see him in this violent exercise to feel all the obligations our theatre owes him, and what combination of physical and mental forces were necessary to introduce movement and life there as he did.[44]

When the *CL* reviewed the 19 April 1774 performance of Gluck's *Iphigénie*, it described the singers vividly:

> Mlle Arnould portrayed the role of Iphigénie as it had perhaps never been rendered at the Comédie-Française, and she sang not only with all the grace that we have known from her for a long time, but even with exceedingly fine intonation, something that is less customary with her. It seems that Chevalier Gluck divined the character and range of her voice perfectly … Larrivée did not sing with less expression than she, but he grasped with less finesse, it seems to me, the spirit of his role. He has more passion than warmth and dignity; we do not find the proud, the superb Agamemnon there. With the most beautiful voice in the world, Le Gros screams at the top of his lungs, but it is impossible to recognize Achille under his bursts: nothing is clumsier, more awkward than his appearance, if not his style of acting. Mlle Duplan would be a beautiful enough Clytemnestre if her voice were more in tune and flexible, but this defect makes us lose several pleasing ideas in her role, or at least hinders their effect.[45]

How far modern perception may be from the original performance of Gluck's works is illustrated by a commentary from the German painter and architect Johann Christian von Mannlich, who knew Gluck well when both were lodging at an aristocrat's mansion. After the initial performance of Gluck's *Iphigénie*, he observed that Le Gros in the role of Achille 'yelled at the top of his voice' and 'threw himself about like one possessed'. As Clytemnestre, Mlle Duplan was seldom in tune.[46] Mannlich also comments on a rehearsal of Gluck's *Orphée et Euridice*, in which Le Gros, overcome with grief at the loss of his beloved, rose and cried in despair— 'Eurydice!'—then fell down again in dejection:

> Gluck was not satisfied with M. Le Gros and had him repeat several times this cry which he always performed in a vocal manner. Finally impatient, Gluck told him testily: 'That is inconceivable! Monsieur, you always scream when you should sing, and when a single time it is a question of screaming, you cannot do it. At this moment, do not think of the music or the chorus that is singing, but scream with pain, as if someone had cut off your leg. And if you can, make this pain inward, emotional, and from the heart.' They began again and Le Gros fulfilled the composer's intention perfectly.[47]

Many accounts, including one from the Swiss writer François-Louis d'Escherny about Le Gros in the 1768 revival of Rameau's *Dardanus*, testify to the tremendous volume of French singers, which most of the public applauded enthusiastically.[48]

20 *The cast and setting*

According to the *CL*, a remarkable change had occurred when Le Gros later sang in Gluck's *Orphée*:

> He sang the principal role with so much warmth, so much taste and even so much soul that it is difficult to recognize him, or not to regard his metamorphosis as one of the first miracles produced by the enchanting art of M. Gluck.[49]

Gluck was also acknowledged as having kept the orchestra and singers in time (relative to before), which was regarded as a rare accomplishment.

Berlioz on Gluck's scores

It is nearly impossible for the modern mind to imagine what was considered an acceptable performance in the eighteenth century. Hector Berlioz, who supported Gluck's music, was amazed when preparing the original materials of *Orphée* for revival in 1859:

> Gluck seems to have been extremely lazy and careless in editing even his finest compositions. Not only did he neglect to correct the harmony with the precision expected of a master; he was not even as careful as a good copyist. Often, in order not to bother writing out the viola part, he indicated it with the words *col basso*, without troubling to reflect that this could lead the violas, which are two octaves above the basses, to climb above the first violins. In several places, for example, in the last chorus of the Happy Shades, he even wrote out all the notes of this part too high, thus producing octaves between the two outer voices ... One can now imagine the type of labour required to restore order in this opera.[50]

When Gluck's *Alceste* was revived in 1861, Berlioz again noted carelessness in the original parts:

> The score and the choral and orchestral parts were in such a chaotic condition ... that every part had to be recopied just as if it were a new opera. It was clear from the slovenliness of the old scores, the absence of indications for bowing and dynamics, the lack of markings for tempo, and the many wrong notes, how careless our ancestors were in putting on operas ... They were not going to worry whether the orchestral players knew what to do—or the conductor, who in those days was rightly called the time-beater ... To edit his works with care seems to have been beyond his power. All his scores were written down with incredible inattention. When they came to be engraved, the engraver added his own mistakes to those in the manuscript, and it does not look as if the composer deigned to correct the proofs. At times the

first violin parts are written on the staff of the seconds ... Elsewhere the composer has forgotten to specify the key of the horns. In another place, he neglects to specify the wind instrument he wants to play an important part—is it a flute, oboe, or clarinet? No one can tell. In still other places, he writes some important notes for the bassoons on the double-bass line, then forgets about the bassoons, and what happens remains a mystery.[51]

In a further commentary on *Alceste*, Berlioz noted impossible demands for the players:

> In the midst of the first chorus of the Thessalian people, whose gentle joy is ... expressed with such charm and truth to life, there is an absurd bit of instrumentation, one horn part making octave leaps and diatonic runs that are unplayable in so lively a tempo. The least-adept musician, on seeing this slip of the pen, might well have said to Gluck: 'Come, come, my lord, what do you think you are doing? You know perfectly well that these octave arpeggios and this kind of rapid phrasing are difficult enough for the cellos and quite unplayable on a wind instrument such as the horn, especially a horn in G! And you cannot be unaware that even if a performer somehow managed to play this impossible passage, the effect, far from being good, would make people laugh.'[52]

In this error, Gluck was not alone. Manuals to help composers avoid the limitations of the wind and brass instruments did not begin to appear before the late eighteenth century, and it took many years for their contents to become common knowledge.[53] Therefore, most composers wrote for them as they did for their own instruments, which was usually keyboard or violin—instruments that permitted much greater fluency. Such parts were simplified, omitted, or thrashed through and lost in the general cacophony that characterized much orchestral performance.

Although Gluck's first opera in Paris (1774) had initially encountered some opposition from assorted supporters of Jean-Baptiste Lully, Rameau, etc., this quickly died down. According to Ginguené, Gluck had no more enemies:

> at least he had none more dangerous than some enthusiastic admirers whose exaggerations offended all of good temper. For example, those who had the greatest pleasure in hearing *Alceste* were not pleased when one made a law of this pleasure[54]

22   *The cast and setting*

Gluck's operas had enjoyed the privilege of being the main fare at the Opéra for nearly three years, but peace and tranquillity evaporated when the *JP* began its campaign against Marmontel and La Harpe.

Notes

1   *Mozart*, 2:397.
2   *DJ*, 615–27.
3   Kaplan, 5.
4   Burney-1, 317.
5   *CL* (May 1771), 9:308.
6   *CL* (August 1774), 10:464. For more on Suard's career, see Darnton, 3–7, 15, 40.
7   Kaplan, 31f.
8   Voltaire, vol. 13, Letter D20828.
9   Ibid., Letter D20905.
10 [Leblond] and *QGP*, vol. 1.
11 *QGP*, 2:541–54.
12 [Leblond], Avant-propos.
13 Some may be incorrect; Arnaud's *Soirée perdue de l'Opéra* was wrongly attributed to Pascal Boyer by the *Almanach musical* (1777).
14 Fétis, 6:84f.
15 *QGP*, 2:231–54.
16 Cited by Isherwood, 238, from *The Complete Works of Friedrich Nietzsche*, ed. O. Levy (New York, 1964), 7:272.
17 [Leblond], 163: 'Ce chant pourra faire aussi les délices des partisans du Chevalier Gluck, mais dans les Concerts seulement, & non sur le Théâtre où il blesse toutes les convenances.'
18 The *parterre* comprised a large number of male standees on the floor. *Cours* may be intended in a 'raid' or 'incursion' sense.
19 *CL*, 11:179. *MS*, 9:18ff.
20 Desnoires, 340ff.
21 *MM*, 2.1 (1785): 418.
22 Published in the *JP* (28 March 1778): 347.
23 *MS* 32:241.
24 Desnoires, 127.
25 Galiani, 256.
26 Cited by Darlow, 132f.
27 Ginguené, 24.
28 Galiani, 478f.
29 Howard, 102–5.
30 Asow, 33. Rousseau quoted in Darlow, 40.
31 Adapted from Asow, 31.

32 Howard, 243. Isherwood, 231. Kaplan, 30f.
33 *MS*, 7:164.
34 *JP* 1777: 10 and 12 February; 2 and 10 March; 8 and 17 November.
35 *MS*, 7:110.
36 *MS*, 7:153. Cited by Howard, 113.
37 Du Barry, 4:271f.
38 Quoted by Kaplan, 148, from *Correspondance inédite de Condorcet et de Turgot* (1883), 165f.
39 Marmontel-1, 42–44.
40 *CL* (February 1769), 8:263f. For the innovations in *Ernelinde*, see Charlton, 378–90.
41 Ginguené, 29f.
42 Desnoires, 93ff.
43 *JPL* (1777/1), 383–85. Reprint in [Leblond], 107–09.
44 P.-L. Ginguené, 'Choeur', in *EMM*, 270f.
45 *CL* (April 1774), 10:417f.
46 Mannlich, 167.
47 Ibid., 255.
48 Escherny, 2:318f.
49 *CL*, 10:473.
50 Berlioz-1, 136f. Berlioz-2, 73f.
51 Ibid., 226f. and 138f.
52 Ibid., 197 and 116f.
53 See Jerold-3.
54 Ginguené, 30.

2 Arnaud's correspondence to Italy

Although the Gluckists always published anonymously, a precise record of Arnaud's technique of deception and lies exists in the form of letters. To support his claim that Gluck was esteemed outside of France by the best connoisseurs of taste and only a few Parisian men of letters failed to appreciate his greatness, Arnaud initiated a correspondence with Padre Giovanni Battista Martini (1706–1784), the widely respected Italian music scholar on whom Gluck had paid a call in 1763 when he presented an opera in Bologna.[1] These letters also reveal that Arnaud's overture was in preparation for the future *Journal de Paris* (*JP*).

In an undated 1776 letter, Arnaud tells Martini that Gluck had honoured him (Arnaud) by putting him in charge of a new journal ('M. Le Chevalier [Gluck] m'a fait l'honneur de me mettre à la tête d'un ouvrage'), which has been undertaken as much for the glory of other nations as for the usefulness of his own. Arnaud hopes that the matters he would pursue and especially his impartiality would induce their illustrious neighbours to furnish him with the means to give his work all the interest and perfection possible. Having devoted most of his leisure time to Italian literature, he is in a position to compare the Italian nation's relationship to all of Europe with that of ancient Egypt to the universe. Although the Greeks perfected the arts, they borrowed from the Egyptians,

> you have always retained superiority ... it is absolutely essential that you help me remove from my nation a prejudice that ... prevents it from paying attention to neighbours whose less pompous merit is in many respects infinitely superior to its own.[2]

According to this letter, Gluck was involved with the forthcoming *JP* to the extent of appointing Arnaud as its director. Subsequent correspondence will show Arnaud's obsequious tone to be a preludial stratagem. Later, he completely reversed his assertion that the Italians 'have always retained superiority'.

Arnaud's next letter of 1 December 1776, requesting Martini's endorsement of Gluck, is quite extraordinary in that it combines an attack on Italian music with extensive praise of Gluck for having corrected these errors. Concerning Italian recitative, for example, Arnaud declared:

> One cannot hide the fact that the interest of your dramas is not found principally in the action; particularly in the action, your music lacks interest. Do your composers neglect recitative because the spectator does not listen to it? Or does the spectator scorn listening to it because the composer neglects it? Certainly neither pays it any attention, and everyone abandons the trunk to cling only to the branches [arias], branches that most often should be pruned. For you will agree with me, my Reverend Father, that most of the couplets [arias] ending your scenes, which we call *airs* and *ariettes*, are incongruous and superfluous parts. They are, however, the only places for which the composer and poet reserve all their talent; and the spectator, his ears. But even when the poet knows how to link these parts to the action, how are they are treated by the composer, and what is found there? Some jagged, wiry passages like the ornaments of Gothic architecture, some rockets, cascades and eternal trails of notes that can display the singer's voice, but disgrace the composer, who is not ashamed to make an aviary of canaries and nightingales from a *Spectacle* meant to affect the soul and stir up the passions.[3]

What could have led Arnaud to believe that Martini would be receptive to such a critique? Although the Italian scholar wished to correct some abuses of Italian opera, primarily singers' over-embellishment, he had no desire to adopt the French design of a mostly continuous recitative, which Gluck represented. In his letter, Arnaud continues the same line of thought about Italian arias when complaining about French critics:

> some people criticize Chevalier Gluck for lacking melody; that is, for disregarding the little details, the pretty little things and baubles. If this criticism had come from this class of men who always sacrifice reason and seemliness to the pleasures of the senses, I would not be surprised. But that people of intellect and letters, these same men who always want the poet hidden in dramatic works, want ... the musician to be visible amazes me. Moved by the great object of his art, he should instead apply himself to hiding the instrument with which he imitates in order to show only the thing imitated. This is what must offend all people of taste.[4]

According to Arnaud, 'these same people claim that Chevalier Gluck is regarded in Italy as a second-rank composer, but I maintain that he is precisely the man you cite in one of the notes of your learned work'.[5] This reference concerned a brief passage embedded in a long footnote in Martini's *Storia della musica* (1770):

> May some *Professore* [professional singer] of rare talent, well informed about all the parts of music, and, above all, about the value and correctness of the harmony and melody, be reborn. Little concerned with the gossip of other *Professori* (who, busy sustaining their own style, scorn everything exceeding their limited knowledge), he will generate, in imitating the Greeks, a rebirth of the true and right action of the affects and lift the spirits of the listeners, already bored with the present music.[6]

In his reply of 28 February 1777, however, Martini did not respond to Arnaud's hint about Gluck as the person described in this passage. Instead, he explained that not all singers were content with Gluck's music because they wanted to show off their voice and its agility by inserting other material. Under the protection of the Imperial Court of Vienna, Gluck made no such concessions to singers [Italian composers did not enjoy Gluck's freedom from the pressures of singers]. Martini cited the much different earlier practice, indicating that the music he desires has not yet appeared:

> In the past, the same deference was not shown to singers. Particularly in their vivid and expressive recitative, Vinci, Bononcini, Scarlatti, Marcello, Porpora and so many other talented Italian composers ... succeeded in arousing extraordinary emotions by means of effective *Modulazione* [composition methods], to the point where listeners would blanch and shed tears.

If this type of vocal music were now combined with the vitality of modern instrumental music, 'what a fine ensemble that would make!'[7]

Despite Martini's silence about Gluck on this point, Arnaud translated his 1770 footnote and appended it to the dedication from Gluck's *Paride ed Elena*, reprinted in the the 1781 'Leblond' collection, implying that it refers to Gluck:

> It will not be inappropriate ... that we cite here the following passage from P. Martini, the most learned musician in Europe, who has been working for fifty years on a History of Music, of which there are already two volumes.[8]

Arnaud's letter to Martini also sought an endorsement:

> I beg you, Reverend Father, to send me your opinion on this point as well as on all those in my letter, and to add to your authority that of the

celebrated M. Farinelli, the learned Accademia Filarmonica, and all the composers and connoisseurs whom you judge truly worthy of being regarded as such. In the present circumstances, you will render the greatest service to our opera, which you will preserve from the shabby, bizarre and Gothic manner [the Italian] that is being proposed for it.[9]

Although Martini's letter above praised Gluck politely a few times, it is primarily a scholarly account of historical and other aspects of French and Italian opera. Instead of opposing Italian music, as claimed by the Gluckists, Martini praised it and its composers, observing that many foreigners (including Gluck) received their training in Italy. Without referring to Arnaud's denigration of melody, Martini cited the positive qualities of Italian music:

> Among the advantages of our Italian music are three qualities in particular that distinguish it from others: melody, harmony and modulations. Italian melody today is subtler than the French and more likely to stir the emotions ... In fact, how did the two great composers and masters from Saxony—I mean George Frederick Handel and Johann Adolph Hasse—achieve such fame, if not by purifying their style in Italy and adapting it to the Italian genius. We know what a reputation the former gained with the operas he composed in Rome, Florence and Naples, after his taste had been formed in Italy. We also know the success of the many works that Hasse composed for various Italian theatres after completing his education in Naples at the school of the celebrated Alessandro Scarlatti.[10]

In the politest manner, Martini left no doubt that he did not share Arnaud's disapproval of Italian opera. His closing paragraph about dissonance seems metaphoric in nature—a commentary on the divisive tactics being employed:

> Allow me, sir, to explain to you a difficulty which I have been turning over in my mind for some time and which, in analogy with what is being done today, deserves very serious thought. I mean the immoderate use of dissonances ... I think that dissonances are and must always have been rough and unpleasing to the ear, because they are discordant by their very nature. I cannot believe that they have today changed their nature so as to become agreeable. Dissonances are only suitable for expressing the most bitter feelings and violent, painful movements of the soul. How is it, then, that one dissonance after another is used to express the most delicate and tender spiritual emotions? This question

has never ceased to trouble me and I submit it to your wise and profound judgment.[11]

Sparse as was Martini's praise of Gluck, Arnaud made the most of it by publishing a 'Réponse du P. Martini' (to Arnaud's letter), with a paraphrased quotation from Martini:

> You have made me, Monsieur, a very just and deserved eulogy of the great talents of M. le Chevalier Gluck. This artist ... has applied himself to exciting the passions and to making the music submissive to the words instead of the words to the music. ... When he composed an opera for the opening of the new theatre in Bologna, I was pleased that he had been able to unite all the most beautiful parts of Italian music with some French aspects and the great beauties of German instrumental music.[12]

At this point, Arnaud omitted Martini's observation that some singers were not pleased with Gluck's work, for they wanted to show off their voices. To his paraphrased quotation from Martini, Arnaud appended the following:

> In the rest of his response, P. Martini treats at length the defects of the old French music and the faults of modern Italian music; on all these points his opinion always conforms to that of the Letter's author [Arnaud's letter above of 1 December 1776, which is printed in full beforehand]. His response ends with some questions about the revolutions and changes occurring so rapidly in music, and modern composers' frequent use of dissonances. As one can see, these questions are absolutely foreign to the object proposed by the Letter's author, but merit being examined; in time they will be made known.[13]

Ignoring the remainder of Martini's letter, Arnaud added a fabrication—that Martini's opinion always conforms to the views in Arnaud's letter. According to the Neapolitan ambassador Domenico Caracciolo's letter to Martini (23 June 1777), Arnaud had boasted about Martini's letter on every corner and published it, claiming full victory.[14] Arnaud's 'Profession de Foi, en Musique', published in the *JP* (28 October 1777), indicates how he used Martini's name and reputation:

> The celebrated Father Martini, who has spent his long life reflecting on and writing about music, has found the union of the true beauties of vocal and instrumental music only in the compositions of this same

Chevalier Gluck, about whom you [La Harpe] speak in a manner so flippant and despotic, you who by your own admission know not even the first elements of the art.[15]

Nothing in Martini's letter, however, could be construed as supporting Arnaud's pretentious claim about Gluck. Nor is Arnaud's characterization of La Harpe accurate.

After learning that the Gluckists were trying to enlist Martini to their side, Caracciolo asked him to support Italian music (10 March 1777). The two letters from Martini to Caracciolo can be summarized as follows:

> 13 May [1777]: Says that Gluck has a special disposition for composing tragedies while [Niccolò] Piccinni's genius lies in the pastorale. Confesses to be scandalized that some want to replace the music of Jommelli, Piccinni, etc. in Italian theatres with Gluck's music.
>
> Undated [1777]: Expresses himself in favour of Piccinni; says that Gluck's operas were seldom repeated in Italy, while Piccinni's ran for months. Distinguishes three styles: the tragic, pastoral, and comic; says Gluck is distinguished in the first, Piccinni in the third, but both occasionally write in the other styles as well. He is surprised to hear that the music of the other authors named above, who have had great success, should be banished, as the Gluckists demand.[16]

It appears that the Piccinnists made no public use of these letters for well over a year until Marmontel reviewed Prince Aleksandr M. Beloselskii's brochure *De la musique en Italie* in the *Mercure de France* (25 July 1778).[17] Beloselskii, who served as Russian ambassador in Dresden and Turin, was not part of the events in Paris. Although he readily acknowledged defects in certain Italian composition and performance, he also cited its outstanding composers: 'For the great masters, [eloquence in music] essentially consists only in the art of moving [the listener] via the melody, and not astonishing with competition by the instruments.' Besides appraising many Italian composers and performers, he mentioned that Gluck's orchestra 'has more force than harmoniousness; and his artist's brush, high-strung to the point of harshness, paints only dreadful things well'. It is true that Gluck's operas were characterized by colossal volume. With respect to Piccinni, Beloselskii wrote: 'Learned in the instrumental part, pleasant and profound in melody, and particularly admirable in expressing the text accurately, Piccinni is regarded as the most perfect of present-day musicians.'[18]

According to Marmontel's review of this work:

> Prince Beloselski's opinion of these two artists cannot please everyone. He will doubtless be criticized for not having sufficiently consulted the true judges of the art in Italy, and particularly the learned Padre Martini, who has been cited to us so many times as the impassioned admirer of M. Gluck's music, and the unrelenting censor of Italian music. Fairness obliges us to make apparent in what and to what degree the judgment of Padre Martini and the opinion of the young Russian [Beloselskii] differ and agree. Here is a faithful extract from Padre Martini's letter, Bologna, 13 May 1777:
>
>> M. Gluck has more talent for the tragic and powerful than for the delicate and tender, while M. Piccinni is distinguished more in the pastoral and comic genres. The latter's music is always mellow, ornamented with lively features, and full of graceful expression; in particular, it is so natural and clear that it is understood and learned without trouble. People even sing his melodies, which, according to the Italians and the most civilized nations of Europe, is one of the greatest merits that music can have.
>> It should not be concluded that Gluck and Piccinni have each succeeded in only one of the two genres, for Gluck's *Alceste* and *Trionfo di Clelia* have some very pleasant arias, and Piccinni's serious dramas have arias of sublime style and great character ... What Gluck's partisans have claimed—that with *Il Trionfo di Clelia* this master prevailed over all the Italian composers at Naples, Rome, Florence, Parma and Bologna—is far from the truth. I recall very well that at the performances of *Il Trionfo di Clelia* in our city [1763], the connoisseurs were divided, some liking his style and others disapproving it. If *Orfeo* [1771] was more successful than *Il Trionfo de Clelia*, it was owing in large part, perhaps more than any other reason, to the beauty of the decorations. [Both operas lost money for the promoters.[19]]
>> I am very offended to hear that they want to banish the music of Jomelli, Buranelli, Piccini, Bertoni, Sacchini, etc. from the lyric tragedy [the Opéra] because it is mannered and of a bad genre, and that the men who pride themselves on taste want to substitute Gluck's music in our Italian theatre. I do not understand on what foundation such assertions can rest. I see these composers' works constantly supported in all the cities of Italy. Even in the pastiches containing only their arias, never, to my knowledge, have those of M. Gluck been included ... I suspect, I admit, that these claims

are a stratagem to introduce German music by inciting quarrels between Italian and French music in order to destroy the latter two. But there is no sign that this project can succeed. It does not seem possible that the Italians and French will adopt the German style, which, however much it succeeds with instrumental music, is an uncertain matter with vocal and dramatic music.

From all that I will draw a consequence according to the maxim: 'Who proves too much proves nothing.' M. Gluck's Paris partisans, not content with praising what is praiseworthy in him, which is no small thing, render him poor service in praising him beyond all measure.[20]

Martini then received Arnaud's wrath in a letter (18 October 1778) asking if Martini and the Italian nation were like those husbands who indeed want to beat their wives but would find it disagreeable if others abused them. After seeing a published letter said to be from Martini, which does not agree with the one Arnaud received from him or the works he had published, he finds only one way of explaining this contradiction:

> The Neapolitan ambassador to the court of France, having learned that you put Mr. Gluck above all the composers of Italy, has doubtless made you see this matter as a crime of high treason and to calm his Excellence, you have felt obliged to recant.[21]

Where did Arnaud get the notion that Martini put Gluck above all the composers of Italy? And how do Martini's published works contradict his letter above? Arnaud's letter continues with his customary praise of Gluck:

> My reverend Father, no one respects more than I the birth, rank and wisdom of M. the Ambassador of Naples, but permit me to tell you that it is worth far more to pay court to the truth than to all the ambassadors of the world. I am not at all German, and when I heard the music of Mr. Gluck, neither my zeal for my country's glory nor my respect for the memory of Rameau, of whom I was admirer and friend, have prevented me from saying loudly that Mr. Gluck is the first dramatic musician to have appeared since the art's renaissance. I have since seen with pleasure that the most enlightened music lovers of Italy share my opinion. To feel the difference between music as art and trade, it suffices to compare M. Gluck's scores of *Orphée*, *Alceste*, *Iphigénie* and *Armide* with M. Piccini's *Roland*. Moreover, the latter had to be retired at the twentieth performance, while M. Gluck's operas ... are always revived, not just with new pleasure, but with new transports.

> On this subject, allow me to tell you that I was more than moderately astonished to learn that in [Gluck's] *Alceste* given recently in Bologna, they had mixed the tinsel of arias [by Italian composers] with this music's gold. This pleases me as much as introducing Harlequin with his buffoonery into the middle of a tragedy.
> Taste thus has neither protectors nor avengers in your country! Be pleased to glance at the Profession of Faith in Music that I addressed last autumn to one of my colleagues [La Harpe], a man of intellect and a good writer, but who has the craze [*manie*] for dogmatizing on an art of which he himself admits not knowing the first elements. Examine the propositions I advance, and, if there is a single one that seems erroneous to you, render me the service of disputing it. In your last letter, Reverend Father, you complain of M. Gluck's too frequent usage of dissonances [Arnaud then defends Gluck's usage] ... Oh! If only your musicians composed in the way that the Carracci's [from Bologna] paint![22]

Contrary to Arnaud's claim, the *Correspondance littéraire* (*CL*) (April 1778) reported that receipts for the first 12 performances of Piccinni's *Roland* exceeded those of any previous new opera. Records assign *Roland* more than 20 representations in 1778, 18 in 1779, 21 in 1780, 10 in 1783, 6 in 1786, and 10 in 1792.[23] With respect to Arnaud's complaint about arias from other composers inserted into Gluck's *Alceste* when performed in Bologna, this practice was common in Italy to make his operas more palatable to the audience. Both Martini and Caracciolo referred to this custom in their letters, and Martini observed that it was done in London as well.[24]

Italian opinion about Gluck's operas is conveyed in this summary of a letter (4 July 1769) to Martini from Gian Francesco Maria Fortunati, opera composer at the Parma court, regarding the upcoming performance of Gluck's *Orfeo*: 'Says he fears very much for the theatre productions, and especially for Gluck's music, which is more mournful than the Lamentations of Jeremiah ... it is written by a master, but without taste and too difficult.'[25] For this performance celebrating the wedding of the Prince of Parma to Maria Amalia, daughter of Empress Maria Theresa, *Orfeo* formed the last act of a mixed spectacle. Recall that Gluck was under the protection of the empress.

Typical of the Gluckist literature is Arnaud's claim that Italy's most enlightened music lovers considered Gluck to be the first dramatic musician since the renaissance of the art. In the rare instance when such an individual is named—Martini may be the only one—it is with false and misleading ascriptions.

In this synopsis of his dignified response (undated, 1778) to Arnaud, Martini indicates that he will not be manipulated by party spirit:

> Expresses his extreme surprise at being accused of favouritism. Says he abhors unfavourable criticism, which is contrary to his nature and religious state. After he was asked to write in favour of Gluck, he was also asked to write in favour of Piccinni, but never said anything against either composer.[26]

'I do not know on what basis I am censured with terms not a little resentful and which offend my honour,' continues Martini:

> Where is there any law censuring an honest, religious man who praises two men of merit ... without speaking ill of either? More and more I am persuaded that party spirit excludes fairness ... in this controversy, I want to do what I have always done (and as you advise me)—to court the truth instead of any person.[27]

Observing that his passage about dissonance did not apply to Gluck in particular, Martini says that he had asked Arnaud's views concerning its use in general. Not having received what he requested, he is dropping the subject. He also enclosed a copy of the letter in question for Arnaud to compare with the printed version. Although this ended their correspondence, Arnaud continued to cite Martini as favouring Gluck (see the 'Leblond' reprint).

In a critique of Beloselskii and as a response to Marmontel's review of it above, Suard's anonymous 'Lettre à M. Panckoucke' in the *Mercure* cited the positive things about Gluck from Martini's text and embellished one statement to read: '[Gluck's] *Orfeo* was highly successful in Italy.' Martini, however, had only said that if *Orfeo* was more successful than his *Clelia* had been, it was owing to the decorations. 'There is certainly no excess in these praises,' says Suard,

> but still they are not as far removed from the enthusiasm of M. Gluck's admirers as they are from the merciless scorn with which he [Gluck] has been treated by his detractors. Father Martini is far from thinking that this is a barbarian to be sent back to the forests of Germany, that those who applaud him are barbarians ... that he has neither song nor melody, that he puts all his expression into noise and his resources into screams, that he has no reputation at all in Italy, that one was very happy not to be deaf after having heard two performances of his operas, and many other fine things.[28]

34 *Arnaud's correspondence to Italy*

When quoting the short passage from Martini's *Storia di musica* (see Note 6) as proving Martini's low opinion of modern Italian music, Suard added a fabrication: 'I could cite other passages from the same work having the same authority, but this one is clear and sufficient.'[29] He further asserted:

> When one reads in the letter we are citing the severe censure that he [Martini] indiscriminately makes of the Italian music so exalted in Paris and all the modern Italian composers, *without exception* [italics added], one is a little astonished, it is true, at the comparison he makes in the letter cited by the *Mercure*.[30]

This again is a falsehood, for nowhere in his letter did Martini censure Italian music and composers but praised them. Like Arnaud, Suard attributed Martini's letter quoted by Marmontel to pressure for supporting Italian music.

Some of Suard's statements in this *Lettre* (such as the 'barbarian' charge) appear to be fabrications, for they cannot be substantiated in literature from the Piccinnists. Others are exaggerations. When a critic praises Gluck abundantly for his positive qualities but criticizes an overuse of screaming, he cannot be claimed to treat Gluck with 'merciless scorn'. That Gluck's operas depended in large part on grand effects generated by an incredible amount of volume from singers and orchestra is well documented. According to the *CL*, singing his roles could require strenuous exertion:

> The exalted role of Iphigénie has put the finishing touch on killing Mlle Rosalie Levasseur. She has spit blood several times and it is feared that she may be forced to leave the theatre for good ... M. le chevalier Gluck could be alarmed if he were not certain of having made us a national music for whose performance France can lack neither talents nor voices. What we fear is that it is at the point of changing singers a little often.[31]

In his response to Suard's anonymous *Lettre* criticizing his review of Beloselskii's essay, Marmontel observed that it is for scholars, artists, and an enlightened public to determine when an individual can be called a great creator. Quoting Suard's words—'M. Gluck will have the glory of having achieved in music what Corneille achieved in poetry: he conceived, he created the true lyrical tragedy ... His place is now assured amongst the few creative geniuses in the arts'—Marmontel replied:

> And who assured him this high position? Who dispensed this glory? Two or three anonymous writers who repeat one another's words and echo one another's replies in the newspapers, in the gazettes, in the broadsheets? These are the voices of fame.[32]

In this conclusion, Marmontel is probably correct. Evidence indicates that the Gluckists' massive writing came primarily from Arnaud, Suard, and Du Roullet. According to Marmontel, writers should identify themselves so that readers can assess the amount of personal opinion involved:

> Anyone who believes himself endowed by nature with the gift of judging everything without having learned anything would be allowed to congratulate himself on possessing this rare gift from heaven; but if, in his enthusiasm, he denies soul and intelligence to anyone who has the misfortune not to admire what he admires or to like what he does not like; if with one hand he seeks to thrust down the statues of the most famous artists and with the other to erect a great monument to the glory of someone whom he had chosen to idolize; his name would reveal if this fanaticism is sincere or feigned.[33]

In sum, Marmontel calls for tolerance: 'In my view, we should now leave the two types of music to contend for the public's favour, for it alone should be the arbiter and true judge.' His article also refutes Suard's various misrepresentations of Beloselskii's text and Martini's views.[34]

Notes

1 See Martini-1, 30f.
2 In Vatielli, 645f.
3 [Leblond], 240–48 at 243f.
4 Ibid., 247. The meaning of the penultimate sentence is expressed with greater clarity in Arnaud's 'Profession de Foi, en Musique' ([Leblond], 396).
5 [Leblond], 247: 'Ces mêmes personnes prétendent que le Chevalier Gluck est à peine regardé en Italie comme un Compositeur du second ordre, moi je soutiens qu'il est précisément l'homme que vous invoquez dans une des notes de votre savant Ouvrage.' A footnote then quotes part of Martini's first sentence.
6 Martini-2, 2:300n.: 'E desiderabile, che rinasca qualche Professore di raro talento, e ben instruito di tutte le parti della Musica, e sopra tutto del valore e della proprietà dell Armonia, e della Melodia, il quale poco curante della dicerie degli altri Professori, che impegnati a sostenere il loro Stile, disprezzano tutto ciò, che oltre passa la loro limitata cognizione, faccia rinascere ad imitazione de' Greci, la vera e giusta mozione degli affetti, et sollevi gli animi degli Uditori già annojati dalla presente Musica.'
7 Quoted by Schmid, 481–87 at 483.
8 [Leblond], 20.
9 [Leblond], 247f.
10 Schmid, 484.
11 Ibid., 487.
12 [Leblond], 249f.

13 [Leblond], 250f., note: 'Dans le reste de sa réponse, le P. Martini traite au long des défauts de l'ancienne Musique Françoise, des vices de la Musique Italienne moderne, & sur tous ces points son opinion se trouve toujours conforme à celle de l'Auteur de la Lettre.'
14 Vatielli, 662.
15 [Leblond], 400.
16 Synopses from Martini-1, 107.
17 Review of Aleksandr M. Beloselskii, *De la musique en Italie* (La Haye, 1778) by Marmontel in *MF* (25 July 1778), 272–86. In *MF* (5 August 1778), Marmontel identifies himself as the reviewer. Writings related to this brochure are reprinted in Angermüller.
18 Quoted by Angermüller, 42f.
19 Ricci, 185ff, 491.
20 Marmontel, *MF* (25 July 1778), 280–83. My translation is based on the French translation of Martini's letter; cf. the Italian in Schmid, 488–91.
21 Quoted by Vatielli, 665.
22 Ibid., 665f.
23 *Pipers*, 4:781.
24 Vatielli, 651, 658f.
25 Martini-1, 254.
26 Ibid., 31.
27 The entire letter in Vatielli, 667f.
28 [Suard], *MF* (15 August 1778), 172–92 at 186f.
29 Ibid., 188: 'Je pourrois citer du même Ouvrage d'autres passages de la même force, mais celui-là est clair & suffisant.'
30 Ibid., 190.
31 *CL*, 12:291f. Cited by Kaplan, 139.
32 'Lettre de M. Marmontel à M. de la Harpe', *MF* (15 September 1778), 161–86. Trans. adapted from Asow, 142–51.
33 Ibid.
34 Ibid., 161f., 182–86. Suard's anonymous response: *MF* (5 October 1778): 56–69.

3 The *Journal de Paris* on the offensive

In its first month of publication, the *Journal de Paris* (*JP*) began its attacks on Marmontel, followed several weeks later by attacks on La Harpe. Unlike today, when political lies and insults can be challenged by a free press in democracies, anyone in 1777 who attempted to assert the facts was in turn demonized by the *JP*. With no countervailing influence present, a large portion of the public believed that anything appearing in print must be true. This chapter examines events through June 1777, including informed appraisals of Marmontel's scholarly *Essai sur les révolutions de la musique, en France*, which was ceaselessly ridiculed in the *JP*. A detailed account from the *Correspondance littéraire* (*CL*), which circulated only to foreign courts and could discuss the quarrel candidly, adds significantly to the literature.

Ridicule of Marmontel

It quickly became apparent that Marmontel was the target of attacks in the *JP* that were designed to provoke a response:

> *21 January 1777, anecdote*: Last week at the Opéra, M. Le Chevalier Gluck's tragedy *Alceste* was given, and Mlle. Le Vasseur played the role of Alceste. At the end of the second act, she sang the verse *il me déchire & m'arrache le coeur*, whose accent is sublime, and someone exclaimed: *ah! Mademoiselle, vous m'arrachez les oreilles* ['you tear my ears'] His neighbour, transported by the beauty of this passage and the manner in which it was rendered, replied: '*ah! Monsieur, how fortunate it would be if you could provide others like it!*'[1]

According to the *CL* (May 1777), the individual quoted was Marmontel and the narrator, Arnaud. The writer then commented: 'To begin a musical quarrel by referring to the ears seems natural enough, but two colleagues, two members of the Académie Française, two encyclopedists! O philosophy, what scandal!'[2] If the remark attributed to Marmontel is factual, it probably refers to the stupendous volume of French singers (recall Mozart's appraisal in Chapter 1). By publishing it, the Gluckists ingratiated themselves with the singers, who held great power, and discredited the individuals connected with Piccinni.

The *JP*'s unsigned lead article on 30 January 1777 is a very short but completely negative review of Marmontel's *Les Incas*, recognized today as a strong plea for tolerance. In contrast, Piccinnist writings always mention Gluck's strong points. The *JP* published long, laudatory lead articles about Arnaud's new works four times in 1777.[3] On 19 February 1777, the *JP* published an anonymous letter attacking Marmontel. After lavish praise of Gluck, the writer concluded:

'Do you know', said someone yesterday in the opera's amphitheatre, 'that Chevalier Gluck is about to arrive with the music for *Armide* and *Roland* in his briefcase?'—'Of *Roland*!' said one of his neighbours, 'but M. Piccini is working right now to set it to music'—'Oh, well!' replied the other, 'so much the better—we will have an *Orlando* and an *Orlandino*'.[4]

Orlando is Lodovico Ariosto's masterpiece of serious writing, but *Orlandino*, by the macaronic poet Teofilo Folingo, is a burlesque parody of some celebrity. The comparison is that Gluck was working on the noble text of *Roland* by Philippe Quinault (originally set to music by Jean-Baptiste Lully), but Piccinni had only Marmontel's reworking of the poem to make it suitable for melody. An account of this *Orlandino* incident was much later included in Marmontel's epic poem *Polymnie*, with Trigaud representing Arnaud and Finon, Suard:

Trigaud, Finon et leur troupe effarée	Trigaud, Finon and their wild troupe,
Pour entasser, non pas des monts altiers,	To pile up, not some high mountains,
Mais les chiffons des plus vils gazetiers,	But the rags of the vilest journalists,
Dans les cafés à la hâte on publie	Hastily publish in the cafés
Que Piccinni n'est qu'un chantre bouffon;	That Piccinni is only a buffoon songster;
Que l'Artaxerce et que le Démophon	That Artaserse and Demofoonte[5]
Sont des Pasquins, sifflés en Italie;	Are pasquins, hissed in Italy;[6]
Et que du chant qui nous est renvoyé	And that the song denied us
L'Italien est lui-même ennuyé;	The Italian himself finds boring;
Que Gluck lui seul charme Venise et Rome,	That Gluck alone charms Venice and Rome,
Naple et Milan; que c'est à qui l'aura;	Naples and Milan, and they vie for him.

Et que Paris, possédant ce grand homme,	And that Paris, possessing this great man,
Veut qu'en despote il règne à l'Opéra.	Wishes him to reign as despot at the Opéra.
'De Piccinni j'ai tiré l'horoscope,	'I have drawn up Piccinni's horoscope,
'Disait Trigaud d'un petit air badin:	'Said Trigaud with a small waggish air:
'Gluck fait *Roland*, Piccinni *Rolandin*.	'Gluck composes *Roland*, Piccinni *Rolandin*.
'Bonne épigramme! au *Courrier de l'Europe*	'Good epigram! To the *Courrier de l'Europe*[7]
'En diligence il la faut envoyer,	'With haste it must be sent,
'La répéter ce soir dans le foyer,	'Repeated this evening in the foyer,
'Dans les cafés demain la faire lire.	'Read in the cafes tomorrow.
'—Le joli mot! l'heureux trait de satire!	'—The fine word! The blissful stroke of satire!
'Disait Finon; pour ce mot précieux	'Said Finon; for this precious word
'Je donnerais ce que j'ai fait de mieux;'[8]	'I would give my best work;'

For political reasons, Piccinni was never attacked in print, but it took place in the cafés and the foyer of the Opéra.

In a further attack (early 1777), the *Année littéraire* published a letter to Du Roullet signed by Gluck (for which no autograph exists), complaining that the Opéra administration had given him and Piccinni the same piece (*Roland*) to set to music. The editor's preface to Gluck's letter reads:

> You doubtless know, Monsieur, that the celebrated Chevalier Gluck was charged to set to music the words of the opera *Roland*. During his absence a vigorous cabal, ever jealous of his successes, engaged M. Piccinni to work concurrently on the same subject. Having learned this, M. Gluck wrote to one of his friends [Du Roullet] the following letter, a copy of which has just fallen into my hands.[9]

According to Gluck's letter itself, however, it was the Opéra administration, not a cabal, that had given the same subject to each composer:

> I have just received your letter of 15 January, my dear friend, in which you exhort me to continue working on the libretto of the opera *Roland*. This is no longer feasible, for when I learned that the Opéra administration, aware that I was working on *Roland*, had given the same piece to M. Piccinni, I burnt everything I had already done— which was perhaps not worth much, in which case the public must be grateful to M. Marmontel for having prevented them from hearing bad music ... I am sure that a certain politician of my acquaintance [Domenico Carraccioli, the Naples ambassador] will invite three-quarters of Paris to dinner or supper to win him proselytes, and that Marmontel, who is so good at inventing stories, will tell the whole

kingdom about the exclusive merit of Sr Piccinni. I am sincerely sorry that M. Hébert fell into the clutches of such people, one of whom [La Harpe], admires nothing but Italian music, the other a librettist of would-be *opéras-comiques* [Marmontel]. They will make a fool of him![10]

Both Gluck and Piccinni had previously set to music at least seven librettos by the Imperial poet Pietro Metastasio: *Allessandro nell' Indie*, *Artaserse*, *Demofoonte*, *Demetrio*, *Ipermestra*, *Antigono*, and *Il re pastore*.[11] Why would Gluck now make an issue of the two composers working on the same subject but with different librettos? Piccinni's supporters had no leverage with the Opéra's administration, which had granted Gluck a near-monopoly for three years. Piccinni gained nothing by working on the same piece as Gluck. The purpose of this inflammatory letter (probably crafted by Du Roullet) was to provoke a response. In his *Essai* published in the spring of 1777, Marmontel quoted part of the above passage, asking: 'And what has this Marmontel done to Sieur Gluck that he should want to ridicule him?'[12] What indeed? The letter signals that Marmontel and La Harpe are the intended targets. According to those who experienced these events, this letter was the catalyst inciting the quarrel. As Pierre-Louis Ginguené recalls in 1800:

> In this war, as in all others, the fault is on the side of the aggressors. Those who find themselves unexpectedly and unjustly attacked have no choice and are forced to defend themselves. Here is what clearly proves that this aggression came from Gluck himself. [He recounts the *Orlandino* episode and Gluck's letter.] One will agree that this hostility was as piercing as it was groundless. It would be useless to seek to excuse this letter, which unfortunately became too public, but perhaps it was printed without its author's participation.[13]

According to René Alissan de Chazet, who edited Marmontel's *Polymnie* in 1820:

> Piccinni worked arduously on the opera *Roland*. It can be reckoned that from the moment (and here the dates are important to establish) that the cabals took shape against him ... the long and obstinate war was provoked and declared ... by Gluck himself. It is sad to see genius resort to such means, and seek to disarm his rival before he has fought ... the day after the letter was inserted in the *Année littéraire*, there were Gluckists and Piccinnists in France.[14]

This letter addressed to Du Roullet, containing inside information and derogatory comments about leading Parisians, had found its way into the *Année littéraire*. Élie Fréron built this journal with attacks on Voltaire and the Encyclopedists, and Arnaud had earlier written for it.

A snare for La Harpe

La Harpe may not have written the music criticism that appeared in the *Journal de politique et de littérature* (see Chapter 4) but did defend it. Its review of Gluck's *Iphigénie* on 5 March 1777 begins with a laudatory passage (omitted in the Gluckist 'Leblond' collection):

> M. Gluk [*sic*] will have the glory of having been the first to find the true plan for the lyric drama. What beauties of all the genres sparkle in his *Iphigénie*! What religious majesty in the role of Calchas in the first act! What expression in this *air* sung by Achille, *cruelle, non jamais votre insensible coeur! &c*. It has the accent of love and reproach, just as this other *air, Calchas d'un trait mortel percé*, is the cry of war and rage. It has been observed that this *air*, separated from the accompaniment, is of the most ordinary simplicity; supported by the instruments, it has the greatest effect [a tribute to Gluck's skill with harmony and instrumentation].[15]

The praise offered to Gluck is longer than the criticism that follows. Mild as it is, it nevertheless drew a swift response in the *JP* from the *Anonyme de Vaugirard*, later identified as Suard, who followed the technique of quoting La Harpe's sentences out of context, omitting key words, and adding derisive comments. On 25 March, La Harpe responded with an article that first praised Gluck's *Alceste* and then continued:

> I have already rendered the same homage several times to the genius of the composer of *Orphée*, and with great pleasure.[16] At the same time, I have reported some of the objections made by those who, also rendering him justice for his fine achievements, do not find him exempt from defects ... I have stated these criticisms with all the respect due to a great artist, and with all the circumspection appropriate to a man who knows only the pleasure that music can bring. An anonymous connoisseur, doubtless more enlightened than I, but whose enthusiasm seems to lead to intolerance, has responded to me in the *Journal de Paris* with a letter in which he treats me with very great politeness and my observations with very great scorn. I shall examine if my observations were ridiculous and if this scorn was justified.[17]

42 *The* Journal de Paris *on the offensive*

As an example of the *Anonyme*'s technique, consider this portion from La Harpe's original review, which follows directly after the section quoted above:

> Those who criticize M. Gluck for often lacking melody observe that Italian arias are still of great beauty when separated from the accompaniment. But it cannot be denied that he redeems this absence of melody as much as is possible by his profound knowledge of harmony and the effects that can be drawn from it.[18]

To this the *Anonyme* responded with ridicule and a *non sequitur*:

> I will not speak of the compliment made to Italian composers, that their arias separated from the accompaniment are still of great beauty. An Italian virtuoso would howl with laughter at the critic if he proposed singing a grand *pathétique* aria of Jomelli or Piccinni without accompaniment.[19]

La Harpe then observed:

> That may be. Apparently in Italy one never sings except in a concert. But here nothing is so common as to hear the greatest *airs* sung without orchestra. In society, the musicians, the *Amateurs* are kind, and do not howl with laughter when asked [to sing], because they are French and they are polite.[20]

The term *Amateur* did not have its modern connotation, but denoted individuals of high social rank. On the whole, professional musicians were held in low esteem because so many had limited training and dissolute behaviour, although composers and elite performers were better regarded. Members of the upper classes usually avoided music as a profession but contributed their services in settings such as private concerts and church. Many had skills that equalled those of the best professional musicians.[21]

In another instance, the *Anonyme* omitted 'perhaps' from a La Harpe quotation, cut off the remainder of his sentence, and then commented: 'In rereading this puerility, M. de la Harpe must be astonished at having let it slip from his pen. It is too easy to respond to this to have any need to do so.'[22] (When writing similar passages, the *Anonyme* also had a penchant for accusing the person he was attacking of being rude to him.[23]) La Harpe rejoined:

> If it is not honourable to cut off a sentence one is citing, it is no more polite to respond in such a way. I leave it to the reader to judge if my

remarks are indeed so puerile ... I gladly recognize the superiority of his knowledge. I ask no better than to be instructed, even at the expense of my self-esteem. But I would venture to offer him a piece of advice: to remove from his justifiable enthusiasm for M. Gluck what partakes of tyranny, to permit observations and critiques to the admirers of genius, and to reserve the tone and expression of scorn for the enemies of talent.[24]

When dealing with an adversary like the *Anonyme*, any argument, no matter how persuasive, will be futile. In quick succession (28, 29 March; 5, 7, 14 April), the *Anonyme* retorted with more attacks on La Harpe in the *JP*, each much longer than the first—a total of 21 pages in the 'Leblond' reprint. Despite the provocation, La Harpe was silent.

On 27 April, the *JP* published a letter from some purported 'Scholars of Senlis' that includes an inflammatory paragraph about both La Harpe and Marmontel (who was from Abbeville):

> The musician from Vaugirard who has written you four or five letters appears to us to be a man of intellect and honour. I am glad that he has played a trick on the fools who would take him for an enemy of M. de la Harpe. A poet dramatist who passed through our town, going to make a play at Abbeville, said to us: This time we are holding la Harpe. He blundered, and I am doubly pleased about it, for we know that he himself is hooted at in Abbeville.[25]

There is almost certainly a *double-entendre* in the quotation attributed to the unnamed Marmontel (see Chapter 4).

Marmontel's *Essai*

In response to these attacks, Marmontel published a scholarly brochure *Essai sur les révolutions de la musique, en France*. Praised by non-combatants for its tone of moderation (in 1781 the *Journal de littérature, des sciences & des arts* called it 'one of the best reasonings and one of the best writings to have appeared in the quarrel'[26]), it was repeatedly ridiculed and attacked in anonymous letters to the *JP*. Claiming at first (3 June) not to have seen it, the *JP* alleged that it was not for sale but was being given away and made various other insinuations about its contents.[27]

A work of serious music criticism that strove to be an objective evaluation of Gluck's strong and weak points, Marmontel's *Essai* sought to counter the Gluckist view that Italian music in any form should be excluded from the Opéra. It also summarized the history of French opera, comparing and contrasting works by Lully, Jean-Philippe Rameau (whose heavy ornamentation required an extremely slow pace, he says), and then the *bouffons* from Italy in 1751. Hearing Giovanni Battista Pergolesi's music made them feel new effects of rhythm, light, shadow, and a unified melody and accompaniment. Nevertheless, many were persuaded that the French language was unsuited to the beauties of Italian music. Although the Lully and Rameau parties united in opposing this foreign music, Egidio Romualdo Duni succeeded in combining true French prosody with Italian composition at the Opéra Comique. His example led to similar works by Pierre-Alexandre Monsigny, François-André Danican Philidor, and André-Ernest-Modeste Grétry. Because these included fine *airs* of noble character, partisans of the old music wondered how to defend excluding them from the Opéra. At this point, Gluck appeared on the scene, supported by a librettist knowledgeable about the French theatre (Du Roullet):

> This new genre [of Gluck] had had the most brilliant success in Vienna; it was even said that it had succeeded in Italy and in England. Indeed, although M. Gluck's *Orphée* had appeared too deprived of song, so that it had been necessary for the theatres of Naples, Florence and London to add *airs* that were not his, ... it is not less true that the form of this production, more animated, more decorated than Italian opera, had pleased, even in Italy. *Alceste* did not have the same distinction, perhaps because of its perpetual monotonous sadness, but it was regarded in Germany as a masterpiece of the *pathétique*.[28]

Continuing, Marmontel wrote that Gluck's music expresses high (*violentes*) passions, such as sadness, fear, remorse, jealousy, and vengeance, which are receptive to screams, sobs, moans, or trembling. The energy of his orchestra makes the voice's *pathétique* still stronger. His music is old French music reinforced by accompaniments of Italian-type church music. Together with a strong and rapid action, it projects dramatic vehemence and heat. This accounts for his success in a languid theatre whose boredom had driven everyone away. Therefore, it was not difficult to reform the nation's taste and ideas, as his partisans claim, for it wanted only music that was less monotonous and dragging than that of its Opéra. But some discerning connoisseurs admired the music of Pergolesi, Baldassare Galuppi, and Niccolò Jommelli, whom Gluck's friends called *the enemies of the talents*.[29] Recall that Gluck's Paris operas depended on exciting the listener with extreme volume. Then Marmontel summarized the matter and described the fears being stoked by the Gluckists:

> With a noisy or thundering orchestra, with piercing or dreadful vocal sounds, do we believe that we have theatre music *par excellence*? Will

the Opéra be deprived of the charms of melody? And will this song, which is the delight of Europe, be unworthy of us? This is what has to be decided, and it would seem reasonable enough to rely on experience. But M. Gluck's partisans do not wish to do so ... They suspect, with fear, that if M. Piccinni has some success, soon his fellow composers and rivals MM. Sacchini & Traetta will arrive ... Consequently, if our ears become accustomed to a facile and natural design, to a harmony as clear in its strength as in its sweetness, to these accents that are not the screams of physical suffering, but the voice of the soul itself, to these elegant, pure designs of the musical period, whose secret the Italians possess, it seems that all is lost.

They hasten to warn us against this seduction. In the journals, in the gazettes, in the evening paper, they never cease inveighing against Italian music, commenting on M. Gluck's music with the same depth as one comments on *l'Apocalypse*, and announcing that his music, revived from the Greeks, is the only expressive one, the only one that is *Dramatique*.[30]

After more commentary in which he cited the most famed European composers (including Grétry and the German Johann Adolph Hasse) as adopting the Italian melodic format, Marmontel reduced the question to determining if this melody is to be restricted to concerts and excluded from the Opéra, as M. Gluck's partisans advised. 'Who will decide?' he asked. The approbation of Italy and all of Europe in favour of this music that had captivated and transported them with pleasure for 50 years should not count for nothing.[31]

Unlike harmonic skill, which can be obtained through study, producing a memorable melody is largely restricted to those few born with this gift. After citing the fine melody in works by Pergolesi, Galuppi, and Jommelli, Marmontel observed that it is easier to scorn this talent than to acquire it.[32] He also drew a corollary about the Gluckists' tactics:

What would M. Gluck have said if upon arrival he had found in the Opéra's corridors a troupe of Italian-music fanatics crying to passersby: 'Don't listen to this German who has come just to toughen your ears with his fracas, in which music, if there is any, resembles a bitter liqueur that burns the palate and blunts the taste?' The German composer, no doubt undeserving of these indecent clamours, would have asked to be heard.[33]

Marmontel's *Essai* also cited Gluck's many achievements. Throughout this work, he abstained from the tone of mockery and ridicule that characterizes most of the Gluckist writings and advocated opening the Paris

Opéra to any deserving composer. Contrary to modern thought, he and other Piccinnists saw much to praise in Gluck's music but asked for toleration of other styles. While the Gluckists claimed that the Piccinnists wanted to import Italian *opera seria*, Marmontel distinguished between Italian music and Italian opera. He criticized aspects of the latter's format and the vanity of its singers, who wanted to display their voices with rapid passagework:

> Certainly this is not at all what we should envy from Italian opera. But are we to be persuaded that these arias, called in Italy *arias di bravura* and designed to show off the voice, are Italian musical excellence and essence? By the consent of the Italians themselves, they are nothing but a vain display and an abuse of their riches. They are not what we propose to imitate from their opera.[34]

Marmontel specified their goal to be simply grafting onto French opera those Italian elements of particular value, including:

> accompanied recitatives, where, without the help of a loud orchestra, a voice (even a light voice) sustained by some chords, conveys to the soul all the sentiments expressed; *airs* of noble and simple character ... and duets and trios in the style of these *airs* ... There now is what Europe admires, what Paris does not cease applauding every day in all its concerts; what it is a matter of admitting to the French Opéra.[35]

Did Gluck really subscribe to the doctrine that arias (*airs*) belong only in concerts, or was it a dogma invented to answer those who found too little melody in his operas? Whatever the case, the Piccinnists' aims were not unreasonable or their attitude anti-Gluck.

The *Essai* misrepresented

The reaction to Marmontel's *Essai* from the Gluckists was uniformly fierce, and its perpetual tone of ridicule cannot be classed as serious criticism. Readily identifiable material of this nature in the *JP*, all anonymous, is as follows:

- 1 June. In a letter on other subjects, elements of the *Essai* were ridiculed, without naming Marmontel.[36]
- 3 June. 'We have already announced this brochure with which we have been threatened for such a long time; which is extolled loudly and distributed secretly [etc.].'[37]

- 7 June. In a brief letter, Marmontel's writing was misrepresented:

   > Today it is published that M. Gluck cannot rise to the musical period, that he knows only how to accompany pantomime, that he has taken the easiest route, that he has been able to succeed only in Germany, which obviously leads to the reproach that we are Germans, and finally that we are all fools or scatterbrains to surrender to the impressions brought about by the alleged bathos of his operas, without knowing beforehand if those that M. Piccini is to give us will be better.[38]

   The *période musicale* is simply an element of musical structure that Marmontel discusses on half of a small page, but it was ridiculed and magnified by the Gluckists into a pejorative term. In derision, some called Marmontel's supporters *Périodistes*. This anonymous writer also appealed to the *Anonyme de Vaugirard* to respond to the *Essai*.
- 8 June. The writer was persuaded that if one were to read Marmontel's *Essai* aloud at the Opéra to the 'ignorant enthusiasts' of Gluck's music, the crowd would vanish in an instant.[39] The term 'ignorant enthusiasts' is the Gluckists' own, an attempt to inflame public opinion against Marmontel.
- 15 June. This 'Analysis of the *Essai*' used the same techniques that the *Anonyme de Vaugirard* employed above on La Harpe's writing.[40]
- 17 June. In a letter purporting to be from a former singer at the Opéra, the irony about the *Essai* is more subtle, and the allusions more difficult for the modern reader to grasp.[41]
- 21 June. The issue began with a provocative epigram 'addressed to an author, who, stung by some lack of success, wanted to get even with the public':

Chez son Libraire	At his bookseller's
Un Auteur mécontent juroit,	A discontented author swore
De composer, dans sa colere,	In his anger to compose
Un Ouvrage qui resteroit …	A work that would remain …
Chez son Libraire.[42]	At his bookseller's.

- 21 June. A letter from a purported 'German gentleman' portrayed the *Essai*'s author as a bigot:

   > But there is among the French intellectuals another oddity of presumption, as ridiculous and more serious in its effects; it is that of scorning other nations and claiming over them a superiority that is unproved and which it would be dishonest to claim, were it genuine.[43]

- 22 June. A letter compared receipts for the Gluck/Du Roullet *Iphigénie* with the vastly lower ones for *Céphale* by Grétry and Marmontel.[44] According to the *Courier politique et littéraire* (London, 27 June 1777), the Opéra's administration had substituted Gluck's *Alceste* and *Iphigénie* for Grétry's work on the days when attendance was highest, leaving him only the days when the hall was almost empty.
- 27, 29 June and 2, 5 July. 'The Brochure and M. Jerôme, a Little Moral Story.'[45] After stating what is said to be in Marmontel's brochure, the author said: 'It is true, one added, that a certain gazette of the evening only laughs at it in an indecent manner.' And so on.
- 10 July. 'Le Gouteux, Teacher of Dance, Story for the Use of more than one Author.' A parody of the *Essai* in which the author is compared to a man with gout who attempts to write an *Essai sur les révolutions de la danse*:

> He had learned some terms of the art, but as the art was completely unknown to him, he used guesswork ... He took one muscle for another, he confused all the genres [etc.] ... his blunders were luminous, his absurdities obvious and his contradictions evident ... Ashamed of having done no more than make himself ridiculous after believing that he had made himself indispensable, he withdrew with rage in his heart and a great project in his head—that of putting into rhyme both his precepts and his resentment—when the gout ... stopped his terrible enterprise, sparing him a new ridicule and the public a new boredom.[46]

Calling this article a 'paroxysm of malice', James M. Kaplan (1984) observed that in his long career Marmontel had doubtless never been attacked so violently.[47]

- 11 July. Extract from a letter from a true German. 'The goal of the [*Essai*'s] author is to conceal M. Gluck's talents from the eyes of the French nation and silence his admirers.'[48]
- 9 September. 'Vision', a parable in which Gluck is the great man, but he will be persecuted, and one will throw against him the *Période*; and I asked what the *Période* was, and the genie told me that it is the daughter of poor taste and envy, but the great man has nothing to fear; he will always be cherished by sympathetic souls, and the multitude will support him; and I saw that the genie was right.[49]

During this period, only one piece in the *JP* might, at first glance, seem to have a more conciliatory tone toward Marmontel. When publishing it on 24 July, the editor claimed that the writer had not previously contributed and that it concerns a true conversation between the author ('A') and another ('B'). Nevertheless, B's mockery of Marmontel and A's praise of the *JP* identify this as another Gluckist letter. The following extracts are typical:

A. I have just read your *Journal de Paris*, which greatly bores me. There is nothing but music in it.
B. Pardon me, Monsieur, if I stop you. I see that you do not like music or humour; but among all the correspondents of this journal, not all are musicians or humourists ...
A. no one reads him. But they read your damned music articles, and that is what is annoying. Sometimes there are some principles and expositions of doctrine so clear that a child can understand them; sometimes some witticisms sufficiently refined, natural and gay to be remembered; more masks than at the ball of the Opéra ... and always the *Période* and the *Essai*. You thus are persuaded that the *Essai* is a good work since you make so much effort to combat it.
B. No one is persuaded of your last statement. With that exception, you say much in favour of the journal—about the doctrine that is comprehensible, some witticisms that are remembered ... these are praises that will never be made of the *Essai* even though we will have established its reputation by mockery. Not to be found there are the qualities of the author, the man of great intellect, excellent man of letters, celebrated writer, who is skilled at inventing a story, who turns verses of ten syllables well enough.
A. Please leave aside the persiflage and tell me when it will please these gentlemen to forget about the *Essai* and end this little journalistic persecution.
B. Since you forbid me to joke about a subject so serious as chansons, I will tell you very seriously, Monsieur, that the war will cease when it pleases the *Essai*'s author.[50]

B thus shifted the blame to Marmontel: 'je vous dirai très sérieusement, Monsieur, que la guerre finira quand il plaira à l'Auteur de l'Essai.' Few people were aware that Marmontel had written the *Essai*, a work of serious scholarship, only after severe provocation. Fewer still had read it. Therefore, the Piccinnists were made to appear as the aggressor, despite the *Essai*'s scholarly tone. For years afterward, Marmontel was portrayed as the individual who had begun the quarrel. Many probably formed their opinion of his work only from the letters in the *JP*.

Not included here are asides in the *JP* about the *Essai* made in the context of other subjects (such as 13 September, p. 3). Moreover, there are doubtless other instances in which the intent and meaning of a passage would be clear only to a reader of the time. Attacks ceased between July and September when Marmontel was out of town. Much of this campaign's activity took place in the cafés, where one could circulate pieces too offensive for print:

Des ordures d'un vieux poëte,	From the ordure of an old poet,
Virgile a fait perle bien nette.	Virgil made a beautiful pearl.
De Marmontel, dit le lourdaut,	With Marmontel, called the lout,
Bien différente est l'aventure;	Fortune is much different;
Car sur les perles de Quinaut,	For on the pearls of Quinaut,
Le vilain a fait son ordure.[51]	The nasty fellow made his ordure.

According to La Harpe, who attributed the epigram to Arnaud, Marmontel kept silent for a long time against this deluge of insults but did compose some epigrams against Arnaud, of which several were thought to be very well fashioned. But he had promised the Prince [Charles] de Beauveau, a colleague at the Académie, not to publish them, and he kept his word. Although he recited them to some people, he never made a copy, and they never circulated. In the same way, the prince had called on Suard and Arnaud to promise an end to the little war and that there would be no more satiric letters in the *JP*. They promised, but the satires continued, always anonymous. These gentlemen disclaimed any responsibility for attacks on Marmontel under the pretext of disputing about music.[52]

When Marmontel saw the letters continuing in the *JP*, he began his *Polymnie*, whose artistic level differs greatly from the Gluckists' writings. The non-controversial section was published in 1787, but the full poem only after his death, in accordance with his wishes. It has had several editions up to the present day.[53] Part of the reason for Marmontel's reluctance to publish *Polymnie* is thought to lie in Suard's threat to 'cut up his face' if he ever did so. In his youth, Suard had carried off all the fencing awards and had some duels, for which he paid with an imprisonment. According to the historian Gustave Desnoiresterres (1875), his threat to Marmontel was improper in that the latter was only defending himself and had rendered Suard important services at the beginning of his career.[54]

In his *Mémoires* written much later, Marmontel explained the unusual circumstances that had led to writing his *Essai* and *Polymnie*:

> I had laid down two principles—one, never to provoke hostility by anything offensive in my writings; the other, to despise its attack, and never to answer. I continued for thirty years immovable in this resolution, and all the rage of the Frérons, the Auberts, and others of the same stamp had not been able to rouse me against them.
>
> Why, then, had I been less passive during the musical quarrel? Because I was not the only person insulted by my adversaries; and

because I had to avenge the cause of an artist inhumanely attacked in his dearest interests.

Piccinni was the father of a large family, which subsisted by the fruits of his work; his mild and peaceful character rendered him still more interesting. I saw him alone, devoid of intrigue, labouring with all his might to please a new nation; and at the same time, I saw a merciless junto furiously attacking him like a swarm of wasps. I expressed my indignation; the junto was enraged, and the wasps turned all their stings upon me.

The leaders of the party had a press at command to print their witticisms, and a journal to give them circulation. Here I was insulted every day. I had not the same advantage for defending myself; and if I had, I should not have liked this pitiful warfare. However, I wished to take my turn at laughing, since to be angry would have been making a very foolish figure.

I conceived the idea of putting their intrigue into action, and painting them as they were. Indeed, to make them ridiculous, I had only to put their own words into rhyme. They printed their prose, I repeated my verses; and every day we tried to see who could raise the heartiest laugh.

Thus was composed my poem upon music, in defence of Piccinni. Perhaps it would have been better had I allowed *Roland*, *Atys*, *Didon*, &c. [his opera librettos], to speak for themselves; but I have not always done what was best; and, on this occasion, I admit that his injury and mine did not appear sufficiently avenged by a contemptuous silence. After all, if I have composed a poem in twelve cantos out of a dispute so frivolous and ephemeral, these are the incidents which insensibly led me on. I might certainly have spent my time better, but my habitual labour required relaxation, and it was these moments of amusement that I gave to *Polymnie*.[55]

Because *Polymnie* is indeed an accurate reproduction of events and verbiage that can be documented, its account of activities in the cafés and elsewhere is most probably accurate.

Informed commentaries on the *Essai*

If the Gluckists had any legitimate complaints against Marmontel's *Essai*, they did not express them in accordance with normal procedures. In 1789, the English music historian Charles Burney evaluated the *Essai* much differently:

> The feuds in France between the Gluckists and Piccinists not only gave birth to daily verbal disputes, but literary. The contention was not left

to the decision of youth and beauty in the theatre, but the partizans of each Music had the venerable assistance of learning and science. I have read, and tried to read, many tracts and brochures that were produced on the occasion, but was pleased with none so much, as with M. MARMONTEL'S *Essai sur les Revolutions de la Musique Françoise* 1778, and M. CHABANON'S *Dissertation sur la Musique* ..., 1785, in which these learned academicians and elegant writers have attacked and defended different sides with all that reason and eloquence can offer.[56]

In the international *Courier politique et littéraire* (July 1777), it is probably Pascal Boyer who wrote:

> In our papers, we have published so many letters concerning the discussions raised in France about music that we believe it will please those of our readers who like to study the progress of the arts to learn that Mr. Marmontel's *Essai sur les révolutions de la musique en France* is available from Mr. Lyde. This brochure, which has made such a stir in France and has just rekindled the musical war with more heat, is both entertaining and instructive, and throws much light on quarrels of this type, for which our paper has so often been the theatre. We cannot recommend too highly Mr. Marmontel's latest work *Les Incas*, a type of moral novel, which is available from the same bookshop.[57]

Until May 1777, this London-based journal had been known as the *Courier de l'Europe*—the one that published the *Orlandino* episode discussed above. But it was impartial in the Gluck/Piccinni matter from at least May 1777 onward, the most important period.

Praising Marmontel's *Essai* shortly after its publication, the *Mercure de France* observed that party spirit enthusiasm, journalistic attacks, the stinging arrows of their critiques, and the jesting of their parodies had not been able to diminish it. After quoting a substantial portion, the reviewer commented: 'It is doubtless difficult to respond to these good reasonings, and not adopt the principles of taste and sound criticism manifest in this work.'[58] On 25 September 1778, the *Mercure* again commended the *Essai*.

An independent assessment

In the *Correspondance littéraire* for May 1777, the events to date are summarized with fluent, vivid writing and sometimes with irony. Although Friedrich Melchior von Grimm had been its guiding force for 20 years, in 1773 he put Jacques-Henri Meister in charge to give himself time for extended travels and other endeavours. The encyclopedist Denis Diderot had often contributed to the journal and had taken over its direction in Grimm's absence. After Grimm's departure from editorial duties, Diderot continued to contribute. Who, then, wrote the following article about the quarrel? It bears the marks of a deft, imaginative writer who is closely acquainted with the major figures in this drama, which makes Meister a less likely candidate. Much later, Meister denied having had any part in this controversy. Back in 1769, Diderot had expressed empathy for Italian music:

> It is to the Italians that we owe the progress made in our music. Some miserable *bouffons* appeared in Paris in 1751, but these miserable *bouffons* made us hear excellent music, and ours—poor, monotonous and timid—freed itself from its narrow confines. The presumption that the melody of Lully and Rameau was the only one our language's declamation and prosody could tolerate vanished, and we have some *opérascomiques* acclaimed in all European theatres.[59]

Diderot took no public position in the 1777 *Querelle* and is the most probable author of *Le Tolérantisme musical* (1779), published under the name of Anton Bemetzrieder,[60] which advocates respect for different viewpoints and granting French composers a greater measure of support. Thus, he would have had an outlook sufficiently neutral to view the unfolding events with the impartiality and sorrow this article conveys.

Because the *JP*'s power silenced most journalists, the *CL*, which did not circulate in Paris, could be more straightforward in discussing the situation. Citing Grimm's well-known allegorical pamphlet *Le petit prophète de Boehmischbroda* (1753), the article begins:

> Where are you, man of God, prophet of Boehmischbroda, the most amiable and truest of the prophets? Where are you, to tell the most distant nations the origin and course of the great quarrel that has just burst forth between the Gluckists and the Piccinnists, and which today divides all the eminent men of our literature? Captivating prophet, I have not your brilliant pen, your saintly eloquence; I am not at all inspired like you. But, to be veracious, is it always necessary to be inspired? If it suffices to be the most humble of historians, the most impartial, the most faithful, I shall be the one.[61]

This reference to the Quarrel of the Buffoons, which took place a quarter century earlier, excludes Meister, as he was too young to have experienced it. Recounting the events from Gluck's first arrival in Paris, the article notes that scarcely any other new operas by other composers were performed during this period:

> For more than four years Chevalier Gluck enjoyed in peace the supreme honour of occupying nearly alone the theatre of the Académie Royale de Musique [the Opéra]. Some attempts to vary the uniformity of this *spectacle* a bit have had so little success that it can well be said that they have served only to adorn the triumph of the new Orpheus. Having been announced as a new genre, it is true that his music experienced at first some persecutions. That had to be: our natural aversion for anything new, except cuisine and fashion, is well known. However, Chevalier Gluck's star soon lifted him over all his enemies. However powerful the everlasting sects of the Ramistes and Lullists may still be in our day, their stunned cabals gave way or at least kept silent. M. le Bailli du Rollet believed that he had impressed the public with a poem he called *his poem*, because all he had taken was the format from Count Algarotti[62] and most of the verses from Jean Racine. The latter were so maimed in the opera that Racine himself would have had trouble recognizing them. Chevalier Gluck imagined that he owed his success only to the creative genius which had revealed to him the secret of a national music adapted to the theatre's grand effects, to the production's general effect, and especially to the particular idiom of our language and poetry—an idiom about which he had acquired profound knowledge in Bavaria and Bohemia. M. l'abbé Arnaud thought like Chevalier Gluck but could not hide the immense services he had rendered to both his country and his friend by the clarity of his commentaries on the music of *Iphigénie*.[63]

A reference to Gluck's first production for Paris, the last sentence is an allusion to Arnaud's expansive praise of Gluck in print. The preceding sentence, too, is ironic. Further, the *CL* observes that purely Italian music had few partisans when Piccinni arrived:

> Thanks to the talents of M. Gluck and his enthusiasts, the direction of the Opéra prospered. If purely Italian music still retained its partisans, they were few in number ... Such was the state of affairs when M. Piccinni came to Paris under the protection of the Neapolitan ambassador. He had been preceded for a long time by the most justly deserved reputation. What reasons to be biased in his favour!—the success of his *Bonne Fille*, however poorly the piece had been parodied and however mediocre its execution; that of all the operas from M. Grétry, who up to then had gloried in being his pupil; and that of all his [Piccinni's] pieces, which had been heard with transport at the Concert des Amateurs and

the Concert Spirituel. His arrival was announced with excitement; our most celebrated artists, our greatest virtuosos, with the exception, however, of M. Grétry, pressed to render him homage. When the Italian Comédiens presented a re-enactment of *La Bonne Fille*, the public clamoured for the composer and received him with more and more acclaim. It was then that the Gluckist party shuddered and the one of Sacchini, Piccinni, and Traetta took a little courage.[64]

Grétry's abstention from the welcome probably resulted from accepting a commission to write the music for *Les Trois Ages de l'Opéra*, whose libretto by the brother of Anne-Pierre-Jacques Devismes (soon to be the Opéra's director) portrays Lully and Rameau in remorse over their shortcomings. Although Gluck does not appear on stage, he is announced by the tragic muse Melpomene as the mortal who had divined her secrets and will offer new glories.[65]

Gluck received strong support from Queen Marie Antoinette, his former pupil. At the same time, she could not countenance public criticism of Piccinni because her sister was married to the king of Naples, the composer's home base. Thus, the *CL* quotes speculative gossip about town:

> It is known that our august Queen—who is interested in the progress of all the arts, and who herself deigns to cultivate several, protecting them all like a precious branch of public happiness—wishes to establish M. Piccinni in France. It is known that the Opéra has given him a considerable enough payment. It is also known that M. Marmontel has arranged several of Quinault's poems to improve their form and musical expression; that he has given one to M. Piccinni, and that they work together every day. What combined circumstances to excite the most vivid alarms! [Now follow quotations from Gluck's supporters:] 'They're preparing a new revolution for us! What tyranny! Incessantly wanting to vary our pleasures! Can the system be changed in music just as in politics? Scarcely were we accustomed to this new music, which at least was nearly as well understood as that of our fathers, said some, when we have to abandon it again! Scarcely had we formed the nation's taste, said others, when they want to plunge us again into barbarism. We succeeded in instilling a grand taste; now they want to give it one of tinsel, all these frivolous ornaments with which Italy herself is disgusted! Is music meant to tickle the ear? It should paint the passions in all their energy; it should tear the soul, raise courage, accustom the senses to the most painful impressions, form citizens, heroes, etc. etc. Let us reunite all our efforts, messieurs, to deter the scourge that menaces both Chevalier Gluck and the whole republic.'[66]

Consequently, the pamphlets, the sarcasms, the little anonymous letters soar from everywhere. By incessantly lavishing upon Chevalier Gluck the most excessive praises, the *Courrier de l'Europe*, the *Gazette du soir* [the *JP*], and all the journals skillfully disseminate the biases most capable of jeopardizing Piccinni's success. He is not attacked overtly, but one tries secretly to destroy all opinions that could be favourable to him. Far from engaging in long discussions, one is content with letting some words escape in passing; a witticism, a malicious stroke suffices. The ridicule that cannot be thrown on the composer is poured out on the poet [Marmontel] associated with him.[67]

According to the *CL*, the above-quoted letter in the *Année littéraire* with Gluck's signature (see p.39) was 'reviewed and corrected by M. Le Bailli du Rollet'. Marmontel did not reply, even though 'he was there treated without respect, and one had the indiscretion of circulating the letter throughout Paris and putting it in the *Courrier de l'Europe*'.[68] As for the *Orlando/Orlandino* insult:

> It would be necessary to have the same genius as the poet of *Orlando* and at least all the talent of *Orlandino*'s poet to paint in a life-like manner the resentment, indignation, and anger that this nasty witticism stirred up in M. Marmontel's soul, the disastrous consequences of this first disturbance, and the misfortunes that could yet result from it, whether for music or for philosophy. This miserable play of words with *Orlando* and *Orlandino* is the first spark that inflames all our literary atmosphere.[69]

Some days after the *Orlandino* anecdote appeared in the *JP*, Marmontel spoke about it in a salon of some 20 persons, saying that only a scoundrel and knave could have used a sarcasm so spiteful and base. According to the *CL*:

> The interest with which M. Suard dared to defend it left no doubt to M. Marmontel about the true author of this clever witticism. Everyone had attributed it to Abbé Arnaud. [Later information points to Arnaud as the author] ... The scene was as vivid as one can imagine.
>
> From this fatal moment, discord has seized all the *philosophes*; it has thrown trouble into our *académies*, our cafés, all our literary societies. Those who would normally seek each other out the most avoid each other. The dinners that would conciliate so pleasantly all sorts of personalities and characters betoken only uneasiness and distrust ... One no longer asks: is he a *janséniste*, is he a *moliniste*, a *philosophe*

or *dévot*? One asks: is he a *gluckiste* or a *picciniste*? And the answer to this question decides all the others.⁷⁰

As noted in Chapter 1, the Gluckists belonged to the religious (*dévot*) wing at the Académie Française, while the Piccinnists were *philosophes* (although this term is sometimes used more loosely). Now the *CL* defines the parties:

> The Gluck party has the eloquent enthusiasm of M. l'abbé Arnaud, the clever intellect of M. Suard, the impertinence of the Bailli du Rollet, and above all else a noise of orchestra that must necessarily have the top voice in all the disputes of the world ... The Piccinni party has scarcely anything going for it except some good reasons, some enchanting music (but music that perhaps will not be performed or heard), the approbation of some disinterested artists, and M. Marmontel's zeal, whose ardour is indefatigable, but whose direction is often more forthright than adroit. To the brochures previously made in M. Gluck's favour must be added the *Lettres de l'anonyme de Vaugirard*, inserted in the *Gazette du soir* [the *JP*]. A persiflage full of finesse and taste prevails there. They are attributed to M. Suard; being the most considerable of his works, it is said that he would be greatly mistaken in disavowing them.⁷¹

The 'noise of orchestra' metaphor refers to the deafening volume of large orchestras. Now the *CL* turns to Marmontel's *Essai*:

> The only writing in favour of M. Piccini to date is by M. Marmontel [the *Essai*]. It is only the leaders of the Gluck party who have not admired its sagacity and moderation. This work has no other object than showing that these gentlemen's learned declamations, their profound and sometimes obscure speculations must not prevent us from opening the course to competition of the talents [confirming that the Gluckists were perceived as trying to bar competition for Gluck]. One will judge M. Marmontel's fairness by the following, which offers, so to speak, a résumé of his brochure:⁷²
>
>> M. Gluck has been well received by the French, deservedly so. He has given musical declamation more rapidity, strength and energy; in exaggerating expression, he has at least saved it from excess by the contrary excess. He has been able to draw grand effects of harmony; he has made our performers sing in time, engaged the choruses in the action, and connected the dance with the drama. His

genre is like a composite order where the German taste dominates, but characteristics of French opera and Italian music are conciliated. Let us give him rivals worthy of equaling him where he is distinguished and surpassing him where he does not excel. May he support himself, if he can, by the strength of his orchestra and the passion of his declamation. May his rivals distinguish themselves by music as passionate and more moving than his, and by harmony as expressive, but clearer and more transparent. And may the nation, after having weighed at leisure the character of the two types of music and the effects they have produced, consider and judge the great matter of her pleasures.[73]

However equitable M. Marmontel's writing, it has served only to irritate his antagonists' party. He has been ceaselessly harassed in all the papers at their disposition. It is a legion of unchained rogues after him, which seems to have sworn to kill him by pinpricks. The idlers amuse themselves, spite revels, and sages deplore in secret the scandal to which philosophy exposes itself ... May someone yet come to tell us ... that it is possible to have different opinions and bear with each other with indulgence! May someone come to tell us that man is not essentially malicious ... There now is the word to send to philosophy's enemies, and what profoundly distresses good souls.[74]

Events several decades later seem to confirm Diderot as the writer of this and subsequent articles in the *CL* about the quarrel. Without Meister's knowledge, part of the *CL*, which heretofore had existed only in manuscript form, was published as *Correspondance littéraire, philosophique et critique, adressée à un souverain d'Allemagne, depuis 1770 jusqu'en 1782, par le Baron de Grimm et par Diderot* (1812). Suard then wrote to Meister, complaining of some attacks against him in these volumes. Because he is scarcely mentioned elsewhere, he must have objected to the coverage of the musical quarrel. In reply, Meister avowed that Grimm's contribution comprised perhaps not 200 pages in these volumes. The first volume and about four-fifths of the second were edited by Diderot when Grimm was on his first trip to Saxony and Prussia. 'Alas!' Meister adds, 'I am more or less guilty of all the rest!' After Grimm returned from his trip to Italy and St. Petersburg (1775), he left the whole business with its expenses and profits to Meister, who writes: 'But until his death [1784], M. Diderot's portfolio never once stopped being at my disposition.' Although Meister acknowledged that others made contributions at times, Diderot's is the one spelt out. 'It consoles my heart a bit', he told Suard, 'to be able to assure you that what wounded you particularly was not from me'.[75] Meister published a response to this edition, deploring the injury done to people still living by making public confidential material that had been intended for foreign sovereigns only. He also revealed his own involvement in the journal, so that Grimm and Diderot would not alone be blamed. In appending quotations from Suard's letter of support, without naming him, Meister called him 'one of my oldest friends in Paris'.[76] There can be little doubt that Meister did not write the articles about the musical quarrel and that he seems to implicate Diderot, who is the most logical candidate.

In correspondence with the Russian court, La Harpe added details about the circumstances:

> With true chagrin I see that this miserable quarrel about music has divided the Académie, in which until then union and peace had reigned. Today it offers two parties facing each other, at the Louvre as in society. D'Alembert, Marmontel, Saint-Lambert, the Chevalier de Châtelux, the Abbé Morellet openly support Piccini, but Marmontel and I are the only ones who have written—he, in the interest of his composer, and I, as reviewer of stage works for the *Journal de littérature*. The Abbé Arnaud and Suard are nearly the only ones supporting Gluck, but they make enough noise for ten and have at their command the *Journal de Paris*, a paper appearing every day. I have strongly disapproved, I admit, the journalistic invectives that both have inserted there against one of their colleagues ... they have not been able to pardon me for having taken the part of Marmontel, with whom I was not at all allied, as if, in discussions so indifferent in themselves or which at least should be, it is necessary to make it a duty to think like one's friends. All the intolerance of their despotism has forced me to separate myself from them, after having spent a long time in their company, which I liked.[77]

Except when it published supplements, the *JP* consisted of four pages—approximately the amount of printed matter on barely half a page of a modern newspaper. On 6 June 1777, the *JP* published a brief pseudonymous letter (from the Marquis de Condorcet, politician, philosopher, and mathematician) about the greatly disproportionate amount of space allotted to music: 'Music alone occupies more space than all the sciences together.' In a factual manner, he went on to cite topical matters with which the *JP* should be concerned, such as slavery. In its customary fashion, the *JP* responded with a sarcastic anonymous letter portraying him as an enemy of the arts: 'I surrender to your sarcasms, and all these little fabricators [*Faiseurs*] and all these cold *Glossateurs* [implying intentional misrepresentation], who dishonour the arts.'[78] This rebuke to a respected individual was an obvious deterrent to any further criticism of the *JP*'s policies.

Notes

1. [Leblond], 102.
2. *CL*, 11:460.
3. *JP*: 13 January, 18 March, 25 July, and 8 October 1777.
4. [Leblond], 111.
5. Operas by Piccinni, 1761 and 1762.
6. After Pasquino, the mutilated statue at Rome, to which lampoons were affixed.
7. A French/British political journal published in London.
8. Kaplan, 116f. My translation.
9. *AL* (1776/8), 321–27 at 321f. This letter was published in 1777 because Gluck indicates that he is answering Du Roullet's letter of 15 January 1777. According to Asow, 85f., the end of the letter contains the following: 'N.B. This letter, written in the confidence of friendship, was not intended, as one can see, for publication. It was printed without the consent of M. Gluck or of the person to whom it is addressed.' This comment does not accompany the original letter, but was an editorial insertion when reprinted in [Leblond], 45.
10. Trans. Howard, 165.
11. Desnoires, 124n.
12. Marmontel-1, 37n.
13. Ginguené, 33ff.
14. Quoted by Kaplan, 30, from Chazet's *Mémoires*, 2:186f.
15. *JPL* (5 March 1777/1), 326f.
16. [Leblond] includes one of these, 107ff.
17. *JPL* (25 March 1777/1), 420–24. [Leblond], 118ff.
18. *JPL* (5 March 1777/1), 326. [Leblond], 113.
19. [Leblond], 116.
20. *JPL* (25 March 1777/1). [Leblond], 122.
21. See Jerold-1, chap. 1.
22. [Leblond], 117.
23. For example, *MF* (5 October 1778), 58.
24. *JPL* (25 March 1777/1). [Leblond], 124.
25. *JP* (27 April 1777), 2: '… Un Poete dramaturge qui passa par notre Ville, en allant se faire jouer à Abbeville, nous avoit dit: Cette fois nous tenons la Harpe; il s'est blousé; & j'en suis doublement content; car nous savons qu'on l'a hué lui-même à Abbeville.'
26. *JL* (1781), 4:163–76 at 169. QGP, 2:541–54.
27. [Leblond], 191ff.
28. Marmontel-1, 12f.
29. Ibid., 16f.
30. Ibid., 17ff.
31. Ibid., 28.
32. Ibid., 53ff.
33. Ibid., 36f.
34. Ibid., 45f.

35 Ibid., 51f.
36 *JP* (1 June 1777), 1f. The misrepresentation concerns the *Essai*, as verified by a footnote in [Leblond], 192.
37 *JP* (3 June 1777), 1–2. [Leblond], 191–93.
38 *JP* (7 June 1777), 2.
39 [Leblond], 220f.
40 Ibid., 194–96.
41 Ibid., 232–36.
42 *JP* (21 June 1777), 1.
43 [Leblond], 198.
44 Ibid., 212.
45 Ibid., 202ff.
46 Ibid., 229ff.
47 Kaplan, 21.
48 [Leblond], 222ff.
49 Ibid., 237ff.
50 *JP* (24 July 1777), 2.
51 La Harpe-1, 2:150 and 150n.
52 Ibid., 150f.
53 Reprint in Kaplan, with annotations and introductory material.
54 Desnoires, 222, 225. Suard's threat is reported by both the *CL* and a letter from Ferdinando Galiani.
55 Adapted from Marmontel-3, 2:110f. See also Marmontel-2, *Livre dix*, 296f.
56 Burney-2, 2:980.
57 *CPL* (1–4 July 1777).
58 *MF* (July 1777), 148–53.
59 Diderot, 'Pantomime dramatique ou Essai sur un nouveau genre de spectacle à Florence', 8:458.
60 A position advanced by Daniel Heartz, *NG* (1980), 'Diderot', but omitted in *NG* (2001). Jerold-2 documents that Bemetzrieder's own writing after he left France for England bears no resemblance to the Paris publications in either style or substance.
61 *CL* (May 1777), 11:456–63 at 456.
62 Francesco Algarotti, *Saggio sopra l'opera in musica* (Venezia, 1755).
63 *CL* (May 1777), 11:456–63 at 457–59.
64 Ibid.
65 Arnold, 82–85.
66 *CL*, 459f.
67 Ibid.
68 Ibid., 460.
69 Ibid., 461.
70 Ibid.
71 Ibid., 461f.
72 Ibid.
73 Ibid., 462f., quoted from Marmontel-1, 57f.
74 Ibid., 463.
75 *CL*, 2:234f.
76 Ibid., 16:213–16.
77 La Harpe-1, 2:153f.
78 [Leblond], 214–19.

4 Libel of La Harpe by allusion

The risk of serious criticism

Attacks on Marmontel almost ceased during the summer of 1777 when he was out of town but continued against La Harpe. Between May and August, the *Journal de Paris* (*JP*) published at least eight articles of negative tone concerning non-musical subjects in La Harpe's *Journal de politique et de littérature* (*JPL*).[1] He was also the target of a particularly vicious personal attack in the *JP* that was meaningless to those unacquainted with past history, but crystal clear to most Parisians. It began shortly after this favourable review of Marmontel's *Essai sur les révolutions de la musique, en France* appeared in La Harpe's *JPL* (italicized text in the first paragraph represents Gluckists' claims):

> The passionate admirers of M. Gluck have seen in his operas a theatre music, *the existence of which Italian composers have not even suspected*, and the only one, they say, which is suited to dramatic poetry. Thus M. Gluck was announced as the creator of a genre that the French opera must adopt *exclusively*, and the music of the Piccinnis, the Sacchinis, the Traettas should be relegated to concerts.
>
>   It is against this intolerant enthusiasm that the author of the *Essai sur les révolutions de la musique* protests. His goal is to persuade the French that they are not at all ready to make a pronouncement about the type of music appropriate for their theatre and suitable for them to adopt; that if M. Gluck's music has great success in France itself and in Germany, Italian music for its part has the unanimous and constant approbation of all Europe … no longer should one defer to the authority of M. Gluck and his partisans, but take time to become informed, and let taste itself, when well enlightened, decide in a natural manner.[2]

Libel of La Harpe by allusion 63

After quoting many passages from the *Essai*, the writer concluded:

> I have neither the intention nor the right to pronounce on the essence of this dispute. The public and time will decide ... But I will observe that the tone and form of this writing which I have just reviewed could not offend anyone. How has one responded? With jests good and bad, by sarcasms injurious to a greater or lesser degree, by journalistic pamphlets whose steady stream resembles relentless pursuit. One can doubtless mix jests with grounds ... but when one becomes more personal and more insulting in proportion to others' weakness [the Piccinnists' lacked a forum like the *JP* with which to reply], then it seems that it has appeared faster and easier to injure than to respond. If M. Marmontel has written only an essay, why wage war against it with satires? Have his anonymous adversaries evidently wanted to prove that to their eyes it was an unpardonable crime not to share their *exclusive* admiration for M. Gluck's music? But they therefore make a party issue of what should be only a matter of taste. *Enthusiasm* is a very good thing, and necessary for experiencing the arts, but *enthusiasm* is only the expression of the pleasure one feels. To order others to have the same pleasure under pain of incurring hatred and scorn is an imperious and revolting fanaticism, and if enthusiasts can make the arts loved, fanatics can make truth detested.[3]

In a footnote justifying using the term 'exclusive' with respect to the admiration for Gluck's music, the writer observes that Gluck's supporters have railed against this characterization, claiming to esteem musicians who work in another genre. Nevertheless,

> they have expressly declared that M. Gluck's music was the only appropriate one for *drama*, that the Italian style can never suit the French *Tragédies Lyriques*, that M. Gluck himself, after having written much in the Italian style, returned to what he adopted in *Orphée* and *Iphigénie*, and that whoever deviates from this route and seeks to write what is called Song [*Chant*] will lack expression, effect and unity [a reference to their claim that *airs* belong in concerts, not opera].[4]

Now follows an episode of chilling audacity.

The *Lettre par DAVID *** son Ami*

Chapter 3 chronicled the *JP*'s attacks on the brief, balanced review of Gluck's *Iphigénie en Aulide* in La Harpe's *JPL*. On 15 August 1777, the

NUMÉRO 227.

JOURNAL DE PARIS.

Vendredi 15 Aoust 1777, de la Lune le 13.

Le SOLEIL se leve à 4 heures 50 min. & se couche à 7 heures 9 minutes.
La LUNE se leve à 5 heur. 5 min. du soir, & se couche à 0 heur. 42 min. du matin.
Rapport du Tems vrai au Tems moyen. Au midi du ⊕, la pendule doit marquer 12 h. 4 m. 1 s.
H. de la Riv. Le 13 à 1 p. 4 p. & le 14 à 1 p. 4 p. | Reverberes. Non allumés jusqu'au 21.

Observations Météorologiques d'hier	Époques du jour.	Thermomètre.	Baromètre.	Vent.	État du Ciel.
	A 7 h. du mat.	15^d au-dessus de 0	28 pouc. 5 lig.	N.	Couvert.
	A midi	23 au-dessus de 0	28 5 $\frac{1}{2}$	N. O.	Clair.
	A 5 h. du soir.	23 au-dessus de 0	28 5	N. O.	Clair.

BELLES-LETTRES.

LETTRE à M. de la Harpe, ou Observations Critiques sur son Journal, par David***, son ami. A Londres, & se trouve à Paris chez les Marchands de Nouveautés; in-8°. de 63 pages.

L'Auteur de cette Critique s'annonce comme un homme qui ne fait que rendre la pareille à M. de la Harpe ; c'est-à-dire, qu'il a été maltraité dans le Journal de Politique & de Littérature : ce qui lui rend d'abord toutes ses Observations un peu suspectes. Il releve, bien ou mal à propos, une trentaine de phrases du Journaliste, & se sert lui même d'expressions fort nouvelles, comme figure rhétorienne , personnifier les termes, des raisons de vérité, tramer des impertinences & des injures, &c. Il auroit bien pu se dispenser de nous redonner dans cette même Lettre de longs extraits du Malheureux imaginaire, & de la Tragédie de Zelmire dont il trouve la versification impétueuse & touchante. Il décide aussi que ces mots de la statue du Pygmalion de M. Rousseau : Moi ! c'est moi ! ce n'est plus moi ! ah ! encore moi ! SUFFIROIENT POUR QU'IL FUT UN CHEF-D'ŒUVRE : comme si un trait sublime pouvoit seul faire une excellente piece ! Les autres articles de ces Observations sont intitulées : Satyres, Amour-propre, &c.

& l'on devine aisément ce que peuvent amener de pareils chapitres.

Ce qu'il y a de moins mauvais dans la brochure, est le calembourg de la gravure qui est en tête. L'Auteur se nomme David ; il a fait représenter dans l'estampe un David qui pince de la Harpe. C'est dommage , diront les Amateurs, qu'il ne sache pas tirer parti de ce superbe instrument !

LIVRES DIVERS.

L'Amour vengé ou Licoris, Anecdote pastorale en vers & en prose , suivie d'une Idilie & deux Odes Anacréontiques ; par un Jeune homme de dix-huit ans , in 8°. de 15 pages d'impression A Paris , chez les Marchands de nouveautés.

Œuvres Posthumes de M. Pothier, dédiées à Mgr. le Garde des Sceaux de France, tome IVe. contenant le Traité des Successions , in-12, de 655 pages, prix 3 l. rel. A Paris , chez P. T. Barrois le jeune , Libraire, Quai des Augustins ; à Orléans, chez Jul. Jean Massot, Libraire, rue Royale.

Quatrieme Lettre de M. Gerbier , Docteur en Médecine, l'un des Médecins de MONSIEUR,

Figure 4.1 Journal de Paris (15 August 1777).

LETTRE

A MONSIEUR
DE LA HARPE,

OU

OBSERVATIONS CRITIQUES,

SUR SON JOURNAL;

Par D A V I D *** fon Ami.

A LONDRES.

1777.

Figure 4.2 Lettre à Monsieur de La Harpe.

JP devoted its lead article (Figure 4.1) to a review of *Lettre à Monsieur de La Harpe, ou Observations critiques sur son Journal; Par DAVID *** son Ami* (Figure 4.2). If an author wished to remain anonymous, as many did, he always identified himself as 'M.***', and never with a *prénom*, which would have been poor form. Therefore, this byline is a red flag alerting the reader to something unusual. According to the *JP*, the *Lettre* is from the one who 'describes himself as *rendering tit for tat* to M. de la Harpe; meaning that he had been mistreated by La Harpe's journal, which makes all his observations a little suspect'. Then follow a few mild criticisms of the *Lettre*, designed to throw readers off the scent of the true author. What the *JP* finds least unworthy in this purported letter is the pun in the frontispiece engraving (Figure 4.3):

> The author is named David, and the engraving is of David who plucks [*pince*] la Harpe. It's a pity, the *Amateurs* [members of the upper classes] will say, that he does not know how to take advantage of this superb instrument.[5]

The following text, quoted from the favourable review in La Harpe's journal (September 1776) of light stage comedies, appears in Figure 4.3:

> *Puns are of old antiquity.*
> *Cicero was fond of them and permitted them in front of the Senate and the Roman people.*

The *Lettre* distorted La Harpe's approval of innocent puns, so that they become the means for attacking individuals' reputations. A peculiar subject for a lead article, the brochure and its review are designed to raise eyebrows. Nine days later, the *JP* published a letter from one Ives-Loan: 'Hurrah for M. David who plucks la Harpe; I will buy his publication, especially if one gives its counterpart, la Harpe who plucks David.'[6] In old French usage, *pincer* has an alternate meaning of being in love with someone. Who is this David?

The *Lettre*'s text of more than 60 pages belies its claim of being from a friend, for sarcasm and ridicule predominate:

> My first plan, most faithful and dear friend, was to analyze your Journal from the time when you began your watch up to the present [5 August 1776 to 5 June 1777] ... and then inform the public of my observations ... but the length of this work discouraged me and I am limiting myself today to a simple letter.[7]

Libel of La Harpe by allusion 67

*Les Calembours sont de toute antiquité.
Cicéron les aimoit assés et s'en permettoit devant le
sénat et le peuple Romain.*

Journal du 5. Septembre 1776.

Figure 4.3 The *Lettre*'s frontispiece. Bibliothèque nationale de France.

Since the writer mocks La Harpe for repeating more than once that he was responsible for only the literary portion of the *JPL*, the music articles in his journal were probably from another whose identity he wished to protect. Now the *Lettre* continues:

> Moreover, you need to be consoled ... It is claimed, I know not why, that you have been afflicted by an enormous decrease in the number of your subscribers. I can assure you that every reader of this letter addressed to you will immediately run to be inscribed on Sieur Pankouke's [the publisher of La Harpe's journal] registers ... Another consolation ... The *Philosophe* must not listen to motives of self-interest; glory is the driving power of great men ... Eh! Who was ever as much a *Philosophe*, as great a man as you? After these marks of my sincere attachment, I believe that you are favourably disposed to listen to me.[8]

After more of the same invective, text about La Harpe is divided into four sections:

Phrases à la Harpe
Jugemens à la Harpe
Satyres
Amour-propre

The writer quoted La Harpe's words out of context and did not identify their location in his journal. In at least one instance, the phrase quoted is not La Harpe's but a quotation from the *Dictionnaire dramatique* being reviewed: 'Par exemple, à l'article *Amour*, l'Auteur observe avec raison, d'après M. de Voltaire, qu'on ne s'intéresse jamais sur la scène à un amant qu'on est sûr qui sera rebuté.'[9] Instead, the *Lettre*'s author quotes this as La Harpe's own words:

> *On ne s'intéresse jamais sur la scène à un Amant qu'on est sûr qui sera rebuté* ... How astonishing that you commit such grave errors! What does this *qu'on est sûr qui* mean? Without protesting the dreadful dissonance of these four words, is the phrase itself French? Do not the two relatives offend against the primary principles? Why use them, since the idea could be expressed more easily and naturally thus? *On ne s'intéresse jamais sur la scène à un Amant* qu'on est sûr devoir être rebuté, ou qui sera sans doute rebuté.[10]

After quoting a *JPL* sentence correctly—'For a long time, it has been rightly said that dancing is the salvation of the Opéra'[11]—the *Lettre* omitted the context, which concerned a brief mention of the Opéra's production of two unrelated fragments: one entitled *Aruéris* by an unnamed composer and the other an act from Jean-Philippe Rameau's *Fêtes de l'Hymen & de l'Amour*. According to La Harpe's journal, the chief attraction of these two compositions was the 'vivid and brilliant expression of the dances and their fine quality, which is scarcely to be found outside of France. This is even more the case since M. Noverre has come to employ these singular talents in our theatre'. From the single sentence it quoted above, the *Lettre* inferred:

> For a long time, it has been rightly said that dancing is the salvation of the Opéra; that is to say, *without the dancing*, the Opéra would be nothing, and this *spectacle* would certainly fail ... If everyone agreed that *dancing is the salvation of the Opéra*, the superior [vocal] talents of Legros, Larrivée, Duplan, Beaumesnil, Le Vasseur, Rosalie, and so many others would count for nearly nothing. Music, this divine art that moves the soul and today makes it feel all the sensations, would therefore lose all its value. Gluck, the immortal Gluck ... would limit his glory to composing some *airs de ballet* ... No, whatever you say about it, it is not at all to the dance, nor the marvels of machines, that the Opéra is indebted for the *Amateurs'* enthusiasm, but certainly to the pleasure of the poems, the excellence of the musical art, and the perfect superiority of its singers.[12]

However, many commentators, both foreign and domestic, agreed that dancing and the visual arts *were* the salvation of French opera. Despite many reports about the poor quality of French singing, the Gluckists always cultivated the singers. The *Lettre* implied that Piccinni's supporters did not honour their efforts.

To the endorsement in La Harpe's journal of Marmontel's work ('*Les Incas* de M. Marmontel seront regardés comme un des monumens distingués de notre Littérature'[13]), the *Lettre* responds:

> M. Marmontel's modest ambition has always been to give the public a work that can equal M. de Fénelon's *Télémaque*. He believed that he had matched it with his *Incas, ou la destruction de l'Empire du Pérou*. This history, which should be called a *history in blank verse*, certainly does not have the right of being compared to the celebrated Archbishop of Cambray's immortal book. There are little episodic phrases stitched one to another; some personages lost from view from volume to volume; a thousand portraits where the author takes pleasure in exercising his pen, which retard the events; a style that is cocksure, disconnected, and full of idle words; an immense chaos of figures, represented grotesquely [etc.].[14]

Today, Marmontel's work is well regarded. Near the end of the *Lettre*, the author again cited the 'enormous loss of subscribers' to the *Journal de politique* after La Harpe became the editor and then continued with more evidence of his conceit (*amour-propre*). After accusing him of substituting his own Greek translations for those of the Abbé Athanase Auger, the *Lettre* asserts:

> In truth, you are universal: poet, historian, panegyrist, translator, journalist, etc ... Every day we see some new talent bursting out in you ... M. de la Harpe, Voltaire the second, good God! ... In its wonder, posterity will place you in the ranks of immortal geniuses ... Someone is knocking at my door, I open, he enters, he reads these last words ... How, antichrist that you [La Harpe] are, he exclaims, do you suddenly prophesy the end of the world, the fall of the human race! ... I hold my tongue and I laugh at the exclamation.
>
> What! It is not *enough* to know Latin and Italian ... you also know Greek! ... You translate Homer, you even substitute your own translation for that of M. de la Mothe! What fecundity! ... or is it rather an additional merit that you would like to place before your readers' eyes?[15]

The 'antichrist' appellation refers to the *philosophes*' freethinking, tolerant beliefs. After another page of ridicule, the author includes an epigram from Jean-Jacques Rousseau, which he says 'can very well apply to you [La Harpe]':

Petit Auteur d'un fort mauvais Journal,	*Little author of a very poor journal,*
Qui d'Appollon vous prétendez l'Apôtre,	*Who claims to be Apollo's apostle,*
Pour Dieu, táchez d'écrire un peu moins mal,	*For the love of God, write a little less poorly,*
Ou taisez-vous sur les écrits d'un autre.	*Or hold your tongue on the writings of another.*
Vous vous tuez à chercher dans les nôtres	*Working yourself to death searching fault in ours*
De quoi blâmer, & l'y trouver très-bien:	*You find only what is very good:*
Nous, au rebours, nous cherchons dans les vôtres	*But we look for something in yours*
De quoi louer, & nous n'y trouvons rien.	*To praise, and find nothing there.*

The 'petit Auteur' characterization concerns La Harpe's short stature. According to Ferdinando Galiani's letter to Marmontel (late 1777), nature had given both Galiani and La Harpe a height of four and a half feet, but they are 'made to do battle at the same rank [as others]'. Now the *Lettre* closes:

> No rancour at all, dear friend, I am only giving back tit for tat ... Go spend some midday hours quietly in your academic arm-chair; go

partake of the repose that you and your colleagues enjoy in the bosom of *mollesse* [indolence, effeminacy]. Members of an illustrious company, sit in the shadow of the laurels and palms that crown your superb heads.
Most faithful and dear friend, I certainly have the honour of being,
Your very affectionate and very faithful servant,
DAVID ***.[16]

Clearly a Gluckist publication, the *Lettre*'s writing style and frequent references to Greek works point to Arnaud as the author. Recall that the *JP*'s review had assigned authorship to someone whom La Harpe's journal had mistreated. Unaware of the great power that Arnaud would soon hold when the *JP* began publication, La Harpe's journal began its 1776 review of Arnaud's *Nouvelles historiques*: 'Nothing is more trite than the foundations of this novel.'[17] The criticism, documented with many quotations, is more severe (but without sarcasm or ridicule) than anything in La Harpe's journal about Gluck's works. His journal published exhaustive reviews documenting faults in works by Claude Joseph Dorat, Louis-Marie Stanislas Fréron, Jean Baptiste Grosier, Imert, Alexis Piron, and others, most of whom belonged to the *dévot* party. This may have fuelled the future Gluckist attacks. La Harpe was probably not responsible for all the critiques, for contributors often wrote anonymously.

A vindictive matter from the past

Arnaud could have felt 'mistreated' by La Harpe's journal, but not any David. In seeing the name David attached to a publication, the French public would have recalled *le bon David*—the term of affection given to the Scottish historian and philosopher David Hume (1711–1776), who was secretary to the British Embassy at the Court of France for 26 months from late 1763.[18] The *Lettre*'s purported place of publication as London, too, would have called Hume to mind. A truly *honnête homme*, he was given the warmest reception by nearly all of French society, except the *dévots*, who did not trust a freethinker. The aristocracy admired him, and the *philosophes* saw a colleague. After an unsuccessful courtship many years earlier, he never married, but always enjoyed the company of women and contemplated matrimony more than once.

After returning to Scotland, Hume maintained close ties with several of his French friends until the time of his death. During his last illness, he wrote a brief account entitled *My Own Life* (1776). After his death,

Suard translated and published it as *La Vie de David Hume*. Because Suard belonged to the Académie Française's *dévot* party, it seems unusual that he should want to publicize the life of a freethinker. Perhaps it was bait for La Harpe, for Suard knew the *philosophes*' deep regard for Hume. Indeed, the *JPL* reviewed *La Vie de David Hume* in May 1777 (without naming Suard or commenting on the translation) as a simple act of respect. A few months later, the *JP* published its insinuating review of the *Lettre à Monsieur de La Harpe ... Par DAVID *** son Ami*. Obviously, Hume could not have written the letter because it concerned events after his demise, but few would have known of his death and fewer still would have read the *Lettre*'s contents. It sufficed to plant the seeds of suspicion in the *JP*'s review, with its 'play on words' and the *Lettre*'s title page and frontispiece. In this manner, both Hume and La Harpe were maligned. Like the letter in Chapter 3 from the 'Scholars of Senlis', where Marmontel is quoted as 'holding La Harpe', the *Lettre* and its review in the *JP* insinuated homosexuality, which was a criminal offence. La Harpe was a widower who later remarried, and Marmontel had a long-term liaison with the celebrated actress M[lle] Clairon before his marriage. That homosexuality was what the Gluckists intended to imply is confirmed by a passage in Marmontel's *Polymnie* in which the character patterned after Suard remarked:

| Je dirai donc que quiconque n'est pas De mon avis n'a pas figure d'homme;[19] | I will thus say that whoever is not Of my opinion has not the appearance of a man; |

At this time, such an innuendo had a sinister dimension. Some years earlier, Voltaire's intervention enabled the journalist Pierre-François Desfontaines (1685–1745), accused of sodomy, to narrowly escape sentencing to the dreaded galley ships. Until 1791 in France, sodomy was a capital crime with a death sentence.

The Gluckists' courting of Rousseau and the *Lettre par DAVID*'s inclusion of his insulting epigram bring to mind Rousseau's strange conduct toward Hume.[20] During his Paris sojourn, Hume found good company in the *philosophes*:

> The Men of Letters here are really very agreeable; all of them Men of the World, living in entire or almost entire Harmony among themselves, and quite irreproachable in their Morals ... Those whose Persons & Conversation I like best are d'Alembert, Buffon, Marmontel, Diderot, Duclos, Helvetius; and old President Henau[l]t.[21]

Libel of La Harpe by allusion 73

Although these *philosophes* had been Rousseau's benefactors, he unaccountably turned against them, accusing them of every treachery. When Hume acceded to Marie Madeleine, Marquise de Verdelin's request to obtain asylum for Rousseau in England, he, too, found himself as the victim of Rousseau's irrational behaviour. In his *Mémoires* many years later, Marmontel recounted this episode:

> But the most astonishing of all [Rousseau's actions] was the monstrous ingratitude with which he repaid the tender and active friendship of the virtuous David Hume, and the deep malignity with which insult was added to injury in the calumnies that he raised against him.
> You will find in the very collection of the works of Rousseau this monument of his shame. You will there see the artful manner in which he prepared his calumny; you will see the absurd proofs by which he thought himself able to convict his most sincere friend—the most honourable and best of men—of deceit, of duplicity, of the blackest treachery ... the following are facts to which I have been witness:
> On the recommendation of my Lord Maréchal, and of the Countess de Boufflers, Hume offered to procure Rousseau a free and peaceful retreat in England. Rousseau having accepted this generous offer, they were on the point of setting out when Hume told the Baron d'Holbach that he was taking Rousseau into his own country. 'Sir', said the baron, 'you are cherishing a serpent in your bosom; I give you warning, you will feel its bite.'
> The baron himself had invited Rousseau to his house, and had paid a great deal of attention to him; his house was the rendezvous of those who were then called philosophers, and, in the full security with which honourable minds are inspired by the inviolable sacredness of the hospitable roof under which they meet, d'Holbach and his friends had admitted Rousseau to their most intimate acquaintance. Now, you may see in his 'Emile' the manner in which he stigmatized them. Assuredly, although the brand of atheism, which he fixed upon their society, had been just, it would have been an odious breach of trust. But with respect to the greater number, he well knew it to be a mere calumny; he knew that the theism of his vicar had zealous proselytes among them. The baron, therefore, had come to know him at his own expense. But honest David Hume thought he saw more passion than truth in the warning which the baron gave him. He made no hesitation, therefore, in carrying Rousseau along with him to his native country, and in rendering him all the good offices of friendship. He believed, and it was natural he should, that he had made the most sensitive and best of men happy; he expressed his pleasure in all the letters he wrote

the Baron d'Holbach, and was constantly endeavouring to remove the bad opinion which the baron entertained of Rousseau ... By every post the letters from Hume to the baron repeated the same praises; and the latter, after reading them, always said, 'He does not know him yet; wait a little, and he will know him.' Accordingly, not long after, he receives a letter from Hume beginning thus: 'You are quite in the right, my lord; Rousseau is a monster.' 'Ay', said the baron coolly, and without any surprise, 'he knows him now!'

How had so sudden a change happened in the opinion of the one, and in the conduct of the other? You will see it in the statement of facts published by the two parties. Here I think it my duty to declare and attest, that, at the very time when Rousseau was accusing Hume of betraying and dishonouring him at London, the same Hume, full of candour and of zealous friendship for him, was attempting to erase the fatal impressions which he [Rousseau] had left at Paris, and to restore him to the good opinion of those who viewed him with the utmost aversion and contempt.[22]

Marmontel's account is substantiated by letters from Hume, Rousseau, and others. After leaving Paris with Rousseau for London on 4 January 1766, Hume spent several weeks finding country lodging for him that he would accept. Rousseau left London on 19 March, apparently on good terms with Hume, never to see him again. On 23 June, Rousseau sent Hume a letter with false accusations of perfidy. Hume then wrote to Holbach, including a copy of Rousseau's letter. Holbach shared it with others, including Suard (then editor of the *Gazette de France*), whom Holbach had recommended to Hume as translator and editor. To Hume's surprise, the details of this incident spread like wildfire on both sides of the Channel.[23]

In the meantime, Rousseau crafted another missive of 38 long pages filled with baseless, paranoiac imputations against Hume's character, dated 10 July 1766. One of these concerned a night en route to London in which they had to share a room in a crowded inn at Senlis. (Recall the insinuation against Marmontel in Chapter 3 from the 'Scholars of Senlis'.) Rousseau claimed that, in the middle of the night, Hume vehemently cried out again and again 'Je tiens Jean-Jacques Rousseau'. In the same room, the third member of their party, Jean-Jacques de Luze, slept soundly through the night. *Tiens* (from *tenir*) is a verb with varied meanings: to have, to hold, to be in love with someone. Alarmed that Rousseau might seek to publish these allegations, Hume wrote on 15 July to Jean Le Rond d'Alembert who read it to a large group of Hume's friends at Julie de Lespinasse's salon on 21 July. After a spirited discussion about the advisability of publishing Hume's experience, they concluded that the public should be informed because the matter would not die down on its own. At length, Hume reluctantly compiled a pamphlet of his correspondence with Rousseau and sent it to d'Alembert with permission to publish it at his own discretion. Believing that the facts would vindicate Hume, d'Alembert had it published as *Exposé succinct de la contestation qui s'est élévée entre M. Hume et M. Rousseau, avec les pièces justificatives* (London, 1766).[24] Because the imprint is false, it was probably printed in Paris, where it appeared for sale in early October. Although the translation of Hume's remarks that connect the text of various letters may be credited to Suard, the *avertissement* is the work of the plural *editeurs*, perhaps headed by d'Alembert. An English translation (said today to have been poorly done) appeared a month later in London as *A Concise and Genuine Account of the Dispute between Mr. Hume and Mr. Rousseau*.

In their *avertissement* for the *Exposé succinct*, the editors noted that Hume had resisted publication until a new development occurred. Rousseau had sent a letter (2 August 1766) of accusation and defamation against Hume to Pierre Guy at the firm of la Veuve Duchesne.[25] According to the editors, Rousseau's letter was conveyed to many in Paris and also appeared in English in London papers. They believed that an accusation and a suspicion (*défi*) so public could not remain without a response and that a long silence on Hume's part would have been interpreted in a manner unfavourable for him. Moreover, this news had spread all over Europe, producing widely diverse judgments. Doubtless, it would have been preferable to have kept this affair a deep secret, but because it was not possible to prevent public interest in it, it was at least necessary to clarify it. After Hume's friends united to present him all these reasons, he finally felt the necessity of the extreme measure he had dreaded so long and consented to have his *mémoire* published.[26]

The fear of a sodomy charge is most likely why Hume's friends had urged publishing. This was no small matter. In England and Wales, conviction carried a death penalty until 1861 and in Scotland until 1887. Rousseau's unbalanced mind not only saw treachery everywhere but also acted on it in the public sphere. After Rousseau voluntarily left the comfort of Richard Davenport's estate at Wootton, he saw an article about his sudden departure that renewed his suspicions about his landlord's view of him—upon which Hume wrote wryly to Davenport on 9 May 1767:

> So you are a traitor, too, it seems; pray, do you speak in your sleep? But you may cry as loud as you please, *je tiens Jean-Jacques*. He has got out of your clutches and is now in the wide world.[27]

The brouhaha that ensued on both sides of the Channel after the publication of the *Exposé succinct* could not have been envisioned by Hume's supporters. With his fluent pen, Rousseau fired back repeatedly (1766–1768), always anonymously:

> *Observations sur l'Exposé succinct de la contestation qui s'est élevée entre M. HUME & M. Rousseau.*
> *Justification de J. J. Rousseau dans la contestation qui lui est survenue avec M. Hume.*
> *Lettre a l'auteur de la justification de J. J. Rousseau.*
> *REFLEXIONS Sur ce qui s'est passé au sujet de la rupture de J. J. Rousseau & de M. Hume.*
> *Plaidoyer pour et contre J. J. Rousseau et le l'historien anglois: avec des anecdotes intéressantes relatives au sujet.*[28]

Further negative references to Hume occur in *Rousseau, juge de Jean-Jacques: Dialogues* and many letters to individuals.

Using a pseudonym or anonymity was commonplace when publishing pamphlets or letters in journals, and a flood of this material appeared in response to the *Exposé succinct*.[29] Perhaps some or many were the product of Rousseau's pen. By writing anonymously and frequently, he created the impression that he had plenty of supporters. After Hume had expressed his concern to Davenport that Rousseau might publish his allegations, Rousseau disingenuously wrote (27 November 1766) to Davenport, thereby deceiving modern readers:

> Whatever may happen, I will continue to leave it to Mr. Hume to make all the noise he wants all by himself, and to keep, until the very end, the silence that I have imposed on myself in this matter. […] I infinitely prefer to be the unfortunate Jean-Jacques Rousseau, delivered over to all this public defamation, than the triumphant David Hume in the midst of all his glory.[30]

This indeed is how Rousseau portrayed himself in his anonymous publications. Now it is clear why the Gluckists sought to enlist Rousseau and his deadly pen on their side. His grudge against Hume inspired the *Lettre par DAVID **** reviewed in the *JP*. From the uproar that Rousseau had wrought, everyone immediately knew this David to be David Hume. As the *JP*'s review points out with feigned reservation, the *Lettre* extols Rousseau's words from his 1772 prose version, *Pigmalion, monologue*, of the libretto for Rameau's *Pigmalion* (1748) by Ballot de Sauvet after A.H. La Motte:

> *Moi! C'est moi! Ce n'est plus moi! ah! Encore moi!*

In the story, the sculptor Pigmalion falls in love with a statue he has created. To his astonishment, the statue comes to life, then reverts to stone before reappearing and revealing her love for the ecstatic Pigmalion in the conversation quoted by the *JP*. These words established the *Lettre*'s subject as sexual and also advertised the new edition of Rousseau's *Pigmalion: Scène lyrique* (Geneva, 1776).

With the above setting in mind and its effect on the individuals targeted, consider the next unusual event. Two weeks after the *Lettre* appeared, La Harpe issued a retraction in the *JP* of his journal's review of Marmontel's *Essai*:

> Taking no part in the disputes about music, I perceived too late and with much chagrin that an article sent me concerning the *Essai sur les révolutions de la musique en France*, which article I included in the last issue of the *Journal de littérature* without a thorough examination, contained some places susceptible to an interpretation very offensive for two of my colleagues at the Académie, known as admirers of M. Gluck's talents. I must all the more disavow everything that could injure them, for nothing would be more contrary to the sentiments I owe their friendship, which has at all times been dear and precious. I ask you, Messieurs, to make public this witness I believe owed to justice, confraternity and friendship.[31]

This humble apology simply furnished more fodder for the satirists. Perhaps the *Lettre*'s vitriol released a flood of emotion that clouded La Harpe's judgment. According to the *Correspondance littéraire*, he retracted because he was refused admittance to some salons. Thus, Arnaud used his women friends to ostracize La Harpe socially, while the *JP* continued to attack his journal.

Notes

1. *JP*, 1777: 19 and 25 May; 2 and 20 June; 7, 22, and 26 July; 6 and 15 August.
2. *JPL* (1777/2), 538.
3. Ibid., 543f.
4. Ibid., 544n.
5. *JP* (15 August 1777), 1.
6. *JP* (24 August 1777), 2: 'Vive aussi M. David, qui pince de la Harpe; j'acheterai son estampe, surtout si on en donne le pendant, la Harpe qui pince David.'
7. *Lettre*, 4.
8. Ibid.
9. *JPL* (1776/2), 98.
10. *Lettre*, 7.
11. *JPL* (1776/3), 240f.

78 *Libel of La Harpe by allusion*

12 *Lettre*, 28f.
13 A reference to *JPL* (1777/1), 232–40.
14 *Lettre*, 47f..
15 *Lettre*, 60f.
16 *Lettre*, 63.
17 *JPL* (1776/3), 297–300.
18 Mossner, 423–506.
19 Kaplan, 138.
20 Mossner, 507–32.
21 Quoted by Mossner, 475, from *The Letters of David Hume*, ed. J.Y.T. Greig (Oxford, 1932), 1:419f.
22 Marmontel-3, 2:6–8.
23 Rasmussen, 137–45, and Zaretsky, chapters 10, 11.
24 Rousseau, *Exposé succinct* 14:279–354.
25 Rousseau, vol. 12.
26 Rousseau, *Exposé*, 14:281–86.
27 Zaretsky, 196.
28 Rousseau, 14:372–416; 14:362–71; 14:332–44; 15:345–70; 14:417–552. Letters in vols. 12, 17.
29 Zaretsky, 188ff.
30 Ibid., 193. Rousseau, vol. 17.
31 La Harpe, *JP* (29 August 1777), 2.

5 The *Armide* episode

At the end of May 1777, Gluck arrived in Paris to prepare his opera *Armide* for its premiere on 27 September.[1] The *Journal de Paris* (*JP*) paved its way with laudatory articles on 4 August and 7, 24, and 26 September, followed by celebratory reviews on 27 September and 1 October. Music for an *air* from *Armide* was published on 29 September. The power that Gluck held at the Opéra was apparent from the unusual conditions he stipulated: at least two months to train the singers and the authority to call as many rehearsals as he deemed necessary. There would be no understudy for any role ('qu'on ne laissera double aucun role'), and another opera had to be kept in complete readiness to perform in the event that any singer was incapacitated.[2] This chapter chronicles La Harpe's final attempt to focus the discussion on facts and the *JP*'s litany of lies and ridicule that followed.

The *Journal de Politique et de Littérature*'s review of *Armide*

Judging from the broad knowledge of opera included in the lengthy review of *Armide* published 5 October 1777 in La Harpe's *Journal de politique et de littérature* (*JPL*), the writer had personal experience in this area. A possible candidate is Pascal Boyer, who in September 1776 had published a constructive critique of the Opéra orchestra in the *JPL*. In this *Armide* review, the writer treated Gluck's works in general and offered his own vision for French opera. In essence, he supported the reform of both Italian and traditional French opera, and praised Gluck's role:

> Doubtless, M. Gluck is a man of genius, for he has composed *Orphée* and, in his other operas, several pieces worthy of *Orphée*. His operas are the first to have been constructed on a plan at once musical and dramatic, whether he himself designed this plan (with which his partisans

honour him), or whether he has followed Calzabigi's plan in *Orphée* and Count Algarotti's in *Iphigénie*. Whatever the case, his operas are the first to be purged of the defects of those in Italy and France.[3]

With respect to Italian opera, the critic observes that Pietro Metastasio's dramas, like those of Philippe Quinault, are very pleasing to read but are not always effective when set to music. Because Italian arias are detached from the dialogue, they too often become a brilliant digression, where the composer displays all the luxury of his art to show off the singer's vocal cords. This is the only thing sustaining Italian opera because the production's excessive length and the too bare simplicity of an insipid recitative do not hold the audience's attention.

On the other hand, he continues, French opera is burdened with a surfeit of ballets, often foreign to the action, and denuded of arias, so that it is scarcely more than an eternal recitative. Gluck's *Orphée*, freed from these defects, could, therefore, succeed in both Italy and France—in Italy, because, aside from the musical beauty, one found, for the first time, a production confined within the limits of a reasonable duration; a drama attracting attention by the unity of interest, despite the faults of verisimilitude; and a stronger recitative more adapted to the drama. In France, *Orphée* succeeded because, for the first time, one heard these expressive arias applied to dramatic situations. Such is the successful revolution that Gluck had created, which must be an immortal honour to him. But in his subsequent works, however strong and fertile the instrumental writing may be, there is little melodic interest, which for music is the most pleasing and rarest quality. He seems to have made a point of banishing melody from the lyric drama and appears persuaded, as his partisans repeat, that melody is contrary to the nature of the dialogue and the course of the action. Although there are beautiful pieces of melody in *Orphée*, the arias of Baldassare Galuppi, Niccolò Jommelli, Antonio Sacchini, and Niccolò Piccinni—these masterworks of the *pathétique* and melody that are sung from one end of Europe to the other, and whose composers express the sentiment so well and avoid the false ornaments so justly criticized in Italy—could offer an object of comparison in which all the superiority would not be on the side of *Orphée*'s composer.[4]

Gluck's lack of melodic invention (except in *Orphée*) was nearly the sole criticism of the new opera form, for the writer agreed on other matters, except the overuse of vocal screams in the execution. Did the lack of good melody in these instances result from the dogma for the drama of declamation, as one might gather from his supporters' writings, or from creative weakness? A gift for melody cannot always be called up on demand. Today, a lack of melody is not the liability it was then, for we have singers whose infinitely superior musicianship and acting ability compensate. In

The Armide *episode* 81

the eighteenth century, good melody formed the foundation of a successful opera (except in France where dancing filled this need). After discussing the importance of melody, the writer concludes by addressing Gluck:

> I am content with your *Orphée*. Since then, it has pleased you to write melody no longer, other than the little that you have allowed. You utilized there [in *Orphée*] this truly lyrical plan, which you yourself have taught us, of a drama interspersed with some arias. You returned to *Armide*, which is a very beautiful poem and a poor opera [not well suited for singing], to establish the reign of your *mélopée* [declamation], supported by choruses and orchestra. I admire your choruses and harmonic resources. I would wish your *mélopée* to be more prosodic and adapted to the French phrase, and less interrupted and noisy [less orchestral volume and fewer screams]; above all, I would desire some *airs*.[5]

In the modern literature, his strongest criticism, which applied not to the entire production but just Armide's role, has been mistranslated and taken out of context:

> From nearly one end to the other, Armide's role is a monotonous, tiring clamour [not 'brawl']. The musician has made a Medea of her and forgotten that Armide is an enchantress, not a sorcerer.[6]

Because a large portion of the French audience demanded unbelievable volume from singers, Arnaud counselled Gluck to exploit grand effects. The educated elite, however, found it boring and repulsive, as implied by the *Correspondance littéraire* when quoting an unspecified source:

> Do you know … why Chevalier Gluck's operas have had so much success in France? It is because [with a few exceptions] his music is French music, as French as it ever could be … he has sacrificed all the resources and beauties of his art to theatrical effect, which should be infinitely pleasing to a nation that has perhaps never been a judge of melody but has the most intense taste for everything related to the drama. To judge if we are right, observe the *parterre* [the male standees], loges and amphitheatre at the first performance of any opera, whether tragic or comic. You will see that most spectators base their criticism or praise on such and such scene or such and such place in the libretto. About the music, you will never hear more than the most commonplace, vague comments. *Cythère assiégée* was a complete failure

because the drama seemed cold and inadequate. If *Alceste* [by Gluck] was very near failing the first day, it was because of the poem's clumsiness and especially the denouement's dullness. After it was made a little less ridiculous, the work was extolled to the skies. And that's how we like music in France.[7]

With most of the audience simply wanting a gripping story, music was an incidental accessory. So much the better if it could raise the pitch of emotion. This is why Arnaud advised Gluck to give the singers plenty of opportunity to cut loose on high notes with astounding volume.

The *JP*'s campaign of disinformation

In publishing the above review, mild and well-founded as it was, La Harpe had committed a grave tactical error. By including any remarks critical of Gluck's music, he had done exactly what Suard and Arnaud wanted by supplying them with material they could turn to their own use. A letter signed by Gluck was published as a reply in the *JP* (12 October 1777), but was probably written by Du Roullet. With misrepresentation and sarcasm, the points in La Harpe's journal are either evaded or ridiculed, and the words twisted:

> I agree with you that of all my compositions, *Orphée* is the only one that is tolerable. I sincerely beg pardon to the God of taste for having *deafened* my listeners with my other operas. The number of their performances and the applause that the public has gladly wanted to give them do not prevent me from seeing that they are pitiful. Of this I am so convinced that I want to redo them. As I see that you favour *tendre* music, I want to put into the mouth of furious Achille a melody so touching and sweet that all the spectators will be moved to tears.[8]

A complete falsification of the review, this passage is typical of the entire letter. Berlioz, who later championed Gluck's music, declared: 'Unfortunately, I am forced to admit that Gluck's defence was as bitter and partial as La Harpe's attack had been intellectual and reasonable.'[9] A response to Gluck signed by one Fabre, who described himself as neither poet nor musician, noted that the composer's words seem to have come from a man of letters:

> One would be tempted to believe that the observations attributed to M. de la Harpe are from a musician and that your letter is from a journalist. These little sarcasms, the essence of the question evaded, all these

subtleties do not seem to be from a celebrated artist. You seek to defend yourself like someone who is in the wrong; or are musicians like beautiful women who want to be loved without scrutiny?[10]

La Harpe's response to Gluck, too, suggested that Gluck's letter was ghostwritten:

> Instead of instructing us, you have amused yourself with mockery ... Mockery is very fashionable. Nothing evinces more spirit, and, above all, nothing better clarifies a question ... I find it very interesting that you have adopted the tone of the *Journal de Paris*, where there is a great deal of mockery for the public's instruction and edification. Moreover, you have doubtless wanted to avenge the German nation for the criticism about its too rigid erudition; therefore you have taken possession of all the honours of French levity.[11]

On 14 October, an anonymous letter in the *JP* rubbed salt into the wound of La Harpe's apology in Chapter 4:

> Does he not know that what M. de la Harpe puts in his journal is not always his own, that he does not always even read the pieces sent to him, on which he makes some notes, and that, consequently, he does not espouse everything he prints and does not think everything he writes. I ask you if it would not have been more honourable to give him time to retract?[12]

A week later (21 October) the *JP* published another Gluck letter: 'Lettre de M. le Chevalier Gluck, à l'Anonyme de Vaugirard [Suard]'. Ignoring La Harpe's favourable statements about him, Gluck again cited him as an opponent and hoped the *Anonyme* would respond to show his friends in Germany and Italy that, among the men of letters in France who write about the arts, there are 'at least some who know what they are talking about'.[13]

This, too, was bait from Gluck's supporters. Why would Gluck publicly appeal for vindication and support, knowing full well that such could only prolong and deepen the controversy? With the *JP*'s extravagant praise, he needed no support. Neither letter is a credit to him, the first being as Fabre characterizes and the second appearing desirous of a quarrel. While they reveal the polished sarcasms of certain French writers, Gluck himself was a plain-spoken man.

Not only did the *Anonyme* respond with a lengthy, harsh personal attack on La Harpe (*JP*, 23–26 October; 32 pages in the 'Leblond' reprint), asserting that he did not know anything about music or Greek, many other anonymous letters in the *JP* heaped scorn on the critic. As for Suard's own qualifications to write about music, the Marquis de Condorcet (among others) observed: 'Suard was completely ignorant about the basic elements of music, and at this time took lessons from [Charles-Gabriel] Foignet.'[14] In his *Polymnie*, Marmontel explained that neither Arnaud nor Suard ('Finon') was learned in music:

'Et vous, Finon, et vous monsieur l'abbé,	'And you, Finon, and you, M. l'Abbé,
'Vous prétendez faire, dans vos ténèbres,	'Claim to make in your dark works,
'Plus que n'ont fait tous ces hommes célèbres,	'More than have all these celebrated men,
'Tyranniser et l'oreille et le goût,	'Tyrannize over the ear and taste,
'Ne rien produire et décider de tout!	'Produce nothing and decide everything!
'Petits régents de la scène lyrique,	'Little regents of the operatic stage,
'Quels sont vos droits? Vous êtes en musique	'What gives you the right? In music you are
'Plus ignorants que les filles des choeurs';[15]	'More ignorant than the girls in the chorus';

As other sources indicated as well, most of the Opéra chorus members, like many of the leading singers, did not read music, but learned their parts by ear.

Very few professional musicians had sufficient general education to write adequately. When the critic who is not a musician by profession makes no judgment about musical matters that can be subject to rules, he is within his rights in commenting on whether the music achieves the desired expression. The *Anonyme* raised a false issue by implying that only a musician had the right to criticize music. Despite his own lack of music knowledge, he wrote at great length about music issues. For the type of criticism in literary journals, writers judged it according to the aesthetics of the period and the impression it made on them as individuals of cultivated sensibility.[16]

Apart from sarcasm, the *Anonyme* was adept at sophistry. Page after page is filled with minute dissection and rebuttal of words in La Harpe's journal. On the surface, it appears impressive, but a closer look reveals seriously faulty reasoning and misrepresentation. In the following passage, the *Anonyme* did not quote the review itself, but falsely claimed:

> M. de la Harpe sees song only in the airs, and melody only in vocal music; he pays no heed that the voice is only an instrument that has its character and particular quality; that a piece of song performed by the violin or flute is not less a song; that the melody, consisting only of a

pleasing succession of tones, exists independently of the instrument used for our ear. It is on this error that nearly all of his arguments are based.[17]

After stating that La Harpe found Gluck strong and fertile in the instrumental portion but weak and poor in melody, the *Anonyme* drew the conclusion:

> As I have observed, M. de la Harpe here regards the melody as the opposite of instrumental music. He has only to consult a musician or read the '*Mélodie*' article in M. Rousseau's *Dictionnaire de musique*; he will see that the melody belongs to the instrumental part as well as the vocal.[18]

To this faulty interpretation, La Harpe replied: 'And I say to the *Anonyme*, with all the musicians of the world and without fear of being contradicted by any, I challenge you to give me a definition of song that I cannot apply to melody.' After noting that these two words are synonymous in universal usage, La Harpe quoted their definition in the '*Chant*' and '*Mélodie*' articles from the *Encyclopédie, ou Dictionnaire raisonné* ('The successive arrangement of several tones, which together constitute a regular song.'), adding:

> If the melody constitutes a regular song, and if the song is 'the manner of directing the melody', I ask if they are not identical. I am informed that melody belongs also in instrumental music. Who can doubt it? Who has said the contrary? ... The *Anonyme* concludes that I 'regard the melody as the opposite of instrumental music'. The opposite! Now here is an expression as strange as the conclusion. No, in all that, there is nothing about the opposite. Nothing prevents combining these two things. I simply said that M. Gluck did not combine them.[19]

There is a type of melody in the orchestral parts, continued La Harpe, but their principal merit (when accompanying vocal music) lies in the beauty of the chords and effects resulting from their combination, properly called the science of harmony. To close his rebuttal, La Harpe summarized:

> I wish that this dispute, which has for its object only the progress of the arts and the perfection of our pleasures, not become more and more an affair of party, a sign of war, and a subject of scandal among those who cultivate letters and who love the fine arts; that those who admire everything in M. Gluck not regard as enemies those who prefer another music; that those of differing opinion in music tolerate and pardon one another, as do those who do not think alike in metaphysics and chemistry.[20]

Toleration, however, was not on the menu for the *Anonyme*. He retorted with a lengthy, serialized letter in the *JP*, several times calling the original review in La Harpe's journal a 'diatribe', and taunting him with having responded four times within 15 days to four critiques published by the *JP*.[21] Two were La Harpe's responses to Gluck's letter and to the *Anonyme*. The other two probably concern very short letters—the first (7 November) correcting a small error of Greek he had made and the second (14 November) announcing that it would be pointless to continue the discussion. This marks La Harpe's exit from the quarrel.

As with Marmontel's *Essai sur les révolutions de la musique, en France*, the *JP* published a series of anonymous letters mocking La Harpe; for example, the verbiage of one on 30 October bears a remarkable resemblance to the 'David *Lettre*' (Chapter 4):

> Letter from One Ignorant in Music to M. de la Harpe. I can even give you an excellent guarantee of my exceptional good nature by telling you what happened to me with respect to your extract from *Armide*; yes, I have to tell you to earn your friendship. I have been the dupe of it from one end to the other; and from your remarks as well as your tone, I would have maintained to Chevalier Gluck himself that his *Armide* was really the most abominable of the *Sorcières*.[22]

The same tone prevails in subsequent letters:

- 31 October, 'Letter to the Authors of the *Journal de Paris*'.
- 3 November, 'Letter to the Authors of the *Journal de Paris*'.
- 4 November, epigram about a *Harpagon* (miser).
- 17 November, letter 'to M. de la Harpe'.
- 19 November, letter signed 'A.B.C. Garçon Apothicaire'.
- 26 November, 'Letter from the Serpent of a Village Parish to M. de la Harpe'.[23]

The *JP* did publish one serious essay (unsigned, but by Arnaud) on 28 October entitled 'Profession de Foi, en Musique ... addressé à M. de la Harpe'.[24] While the tone is more elevated, the entire essay offered a one-sided view of Italian opera's worst features, falsely implying that La Harpe advocated importing it.

Arnaud's view of Italian opera is expressed in a small tract attributed to him, *La soirée perdue à l'opéra* (1776, before the *JP* began publication), in which he employed a conversational style to refute some purported objections to Gluck's music in *Alceste*:

- I admit, says a young man, that ... I would be tempted to believe that Chevalier Gluck's style is indeed more animated and theatrical than that of the other composers; but what kind of opera is it where there is no melody at all?
- Ah! Barbarian ... A thousand pardons, Monsieur, for my hastiness. I didn't mean to offend you. You find, therefore, that there is no melody at all in this opera? Could it be because there are neither chansonettes, nor noëls, nor brunettes, nor vaudevilles, nor cantiques [all light, popular songs], nor drinking songs?
- But here, I want something other than what I hear ...
- Ah! Monsieur, in the name of Apollo and all the Muses, leave to Italian music the pretentious ornaments, tinsel and extravagances that have dishonoured it for too long a time. Guard against envying false and worthless riches, and do not appeal to a manner proscribed everywhere there are philosophers, people of intellect, and enlightened connoisseurs in Italy. What! You find it good that at the same moment when your soul is carried to the highest degree of emotion for which it has been prepared, the singer amuses himself by embroidering some vowels, and, as if by a spell, leaves his mouth open in the middle of a word to let a multitude of unarticulated sounds pour forth![25]

Arnaud portrayed an abuse of Italian opera as if it were an integral part of it. As the *Correspondance littéraire* observed: 'No one is asking from M. Gluck trills, appoggiaturas, roulades and all these little ornaments that good taste disdains.' What they were asking is something quite different:

> It is necessary to know how to rend the heart without wounding the ear and taste. If some cries alone [Gluck's abundant use of high volume] could determine the worth of a dramatic work, there is perhaps not one piece of M. Sedaine that should not prevail over all the masterworks of Voltaire and Racine. In evaluating the talents of musicians, why not follow the same logic that one would certainly follow in appraising a poet?[26]

During *Armide*'s run at the Opéra, Sacchini's *Olympiade* at the Italian theatre became popular so quickly, says the *Mémoires secrets*, that the Gluckists had to take action:

> Although *Olympiade* was horribly executed and sung at the Italian theatre, the connoisseurs and people of taste had nonetheless discerned the music's beauty, which they found greatly superior to that of *Armide*, especially for melody. Chevalier Gluck and his partisans, furious at

this preference, aroused the Opéra's jealousy, which, taking advantage of its *privilège*, claimed that the Comédie Italienne was encroaching on it and could not perform works in which there were choruses and more than seven singers on stage. Consequently, there was recourse to authority, which halted *Olympiade* after the fourth performance. This infamy revolted all Paris. The injustice is all the more appalling in that this lyric drama was accepted by the Italian theatre only after the Opéra directors, having studied and rehearsed it, rejected it for fear of displeasing Chevalier Gluck and the Gluckists. It reflects great discredit on the German, whose base schemes were clearly displayed on this occasion.[27]

Olympiade's success was all the more striking because it is a serious opera, not the comic opera usually offered at the Italian theatre.[28] This episode was reported also by the *Correspondance littéraire* (November 1777). For once, the *JP* was uncharacteristically silent.

Another assessment

According to the *Correspondance littéraire*'s report about Gluck's *Armide*, this production, which was to have been decisive and had been impatiently awaited by both parties for a long time, had decided nothing. The Gluckists and Piccinnists still retained the same aversions, the same pretensions, and the same fury, but the first performance could alarm the less zealous partisans for M. Gluck's cause:

> Nearly the entire opera was heard with great indifference; only the end of the first act and some airs of the fourth act attracted some strong applause. Most spectators ventured to admit that, of all M. Gluck's works, this one had given them the least pleasure. It is said that he wanted to work in a genre not his own. He used might and energy where only grace and softness were required. Except for the choruses and some grand orchestral effects, there are few scenes where one is not tempted to miss the facile and natural melody of the good Lulli [whose setting of *Armide* (1686) was still well known], etc.
>
> Up to this point, M. de La Harpe had not yet dared take part in this famous quarrel; at least, he had said in his journal only some words in favour of M. Marmontel's brochure. But he quietly disavowed them two days later in the *Feuille du soir* [the *JP*] to appease several women of his acquaintance whose doors were closed to him because of this indiscretion. In spite of such a harsh lesson ... M. de La Harpe ventured to prepare in connection with *Armide* a very lengthy and

severe critique of M. Gluck's whole musical system [the writer imitates Gluckist exaggeration as a form of wit]. There he expatiated as far as the eye can see on the harmony and melody, on the song and accompaniments, on the recitative and *mélopée*. Could one let such a great audacity go unpunished? *M. le chevalier* did not fail to cry injustice. He began by mocking his new Aristarch quite briskly. Then he appealed for help from all men of letters who are able to feel and explain his art's secrets. He made it understood that it was a matter of avenging the glory of the nation, of teaching foreigners that all our writers are not as ignorant as M. de La Harpe. He addressed himself most particularly to the *Anonyme de Vaugirard*. This *Anonyme* is, as everyone knows, M. Suard, who did not refuse the pleasure of taking up the cudgels with M. de La Harpe for the honour of German music.[29]

In reality, most of the *JPL* review quoted above either praises Gluck or is completely neutral when supplying lengthy background information. Instead of two parties engaged in serious debate, one intended only to bait the other. In his letter to the Russian court shortly before the staging of *Armide*, La Harpe observed the Gluckists' lack of sincere intent:

> No one has yet responded to Marmontel's letter [the *Essai*] with anything but sarcasms, which only shows the difficulty of making a suitable serious return. They [the sarcasms] are inserted daily in a paper called the *Journal de Paris*, which is a very favourable setting for these small polemical writings because it appears every day and one blow follows another. S** [Suard], who has already responded to me, and harshly enough, is also the one who has skirmished against Marmontel. But the more spirit and taste for it he has, the less I pardon him for avoiding the question and making only a quarrel of it.[30]

Notes

1 Libretto by Philippe Quinault after Torquato Tasso, originally set to music by Jean-Baptiste Lully.
2 *EMM*, 1:626.
3 *JPL* (5 October 1777/3), 163–70 at 166. [Leblond], 259–70 at 263f.
4 Ibid.
5 Ibid., 169f. [Leblond], 269f.
6 Ibid., 165. [Leblond], 261.
7 *CL* (May 1777), 11:458.
8 'Lettre de M. le Chevalier Gluck à M. de La Harpe', *JP* (12 October 1777). [Leblond], 271–75 at 272f.

9   Desnoires, 210f. Berlioz, *Gazette musicale de Paris* (1 June 1834), rpt. in Berlioz-3, 1:250.
10 *JP* (16 October 1777). [Leblond], 276.
11 *JPL* (25 October 1777/3), 260f.
12 *JP* (14 October 1777), 2f.
13 [Leblond], 280f.
14 Quoted by Desnoires, 269, from Condorcet's *Mémoires sur la Révolution française* (Paris, 1824), 1:64.
15 Kaplan, 119. My translation.
16 See Le Pileur d'Apligny, *Traité sur la musique* (Paris, 1779), 156f.
17 [Leblond], 292.
18 Ibid.
19 *JPL* (5 November 1777/3), 296–310. [Leblond], 348f.
20 Ibid.
21 *JP* (9–11 November 1777). [Leblond], 354–74.
22 [Leblond], 317f.
23 Except the 19 November letter, all are in [Leblond], 319, 350, 379, 384.
24 [Leblond], 396–401.
25 [Arnaud], 9–12.
26 *CL* (May 1776), 11:261f.
27 *MS* (12 October 1777), 10:245.
28 Isherwood, 239 and the Piccinni chapters in Desnoiresterres document later Gluckist tactics.
29 *CL* (September 1777), 11:537f.
30 La Harpe-1, 2:116f.

6 Piccinni's opera and further events

After a full year of attacks on Italian music and its supporters, Piccinni's work still had not been heard. Now the focus can turn to the long-awaited production of his opera *Roland*, the influence and identity of the Mélophile, the intimidation of journalists, and the techniques used to sow discord in society and silence critics.

Piccinni's *Roland*

Arriving in Paris late in 1776, Piccinni spent a year working with his librettist Marmontel on *Roland*, a *tragédie lyrique* presented at the Paris Opéra on 27 January 1778. Justifiably, his supporters viewed the campaign of ridicule against Marmontel and La Harpe as an attempt to silence them and Italian music. The issue, the right for Piccinni to present his music, was an artificial one contrived by the Gluckists to incite a quarrel for the purpose of assuring Gluck's supremacy at the Opéra and the financial success of the *Journal de Paris* (*JP*). In 1800 Pierre-Louis Ginguené described the effect of all this verbiage:

> The war of the pen provoked in this way [by Gluck's first letter, see p.39] soon blazed. The exaggeration to which Gluck's admirers devoted themselves produced exaggerated feelings, in a contrary sense, in those who did not share their admiration. The animosity associated with the Italians, the Italian period, Italian melodies, and Piccinni (who, being Italian, was censured in advance, together with his melodies and his periods)—all that irritated even those who, not knowing him but knowing good Italian music ... found in this abuse only party spirit, fanaticism, ignorance and bad faith. Those who saw him up close suffered still more impatiently these blind judgments, these ridiculous prejudices, this unjust and disheartening disparagement. Piccinni's character, his social qualities, his simple and retiring life ... his philosophy,

rare in men of his art and country, his modest pride, which rendered him equally incapable of self-praise and debasement; finally, everything concerning him as a man and artist did not dispose them to view with patience all that was done in advance to arm opinion against a work that did not yet exist.[1]

As Ginguené relates, the writings described above inflamed tempers and made a public, already barely capable of making a good judgment about these matters, absolutely unable to judge them soundly. While Marmontel had wanted his *Essai sur les révolutions de la musique, en France* to bring attention back to the essential heart of the matter (the right to hear Italian music at the Opéra), he succeeded only in further irritating sentiment against both himself and the peaceable composer of *Roland*. Soon rehearsals for Piccinni's opera began, and the partisans and enemies prepared their arms. The latter seemed stronger because they were the loudest. As the performance approached, they became more so.[2] According to the *Correspondance littéraire*:

> There has never been an opera whose rehearsals have been more troublesome, more tumultuous, or noisier than those of *Roland*. The singers and orchestra, equally strangers to the new musical genre, constantly lost the beat, and sometimes fell again into the sudden screams associated with Gluck's music and sometimes into the heavy, dragging psalmody of the good Lully. No one knew to whom to listen. Although the Chevalier Gluck had used the most grandiose gestures to wind up the discordant machine [for his operas], his competitor and rival remained quietly in a corner of the theatre, despairing inaudibly to himself ... M. Marmontel, meanwhile, was stumped. He pressed and tormented his friend Piccini not to give up: 'And show them then the right tempo of this *air*—you see that they do not get it.' Piccini raised his eyes to heaven and responded meekly: 'Ah! Everything is going badly! Everything.'[3]

Although it seems that French composers usually did not participate to any great extent in rehearsals, Gluck's active role in coaching the singers is confirmed by the neutral *Courier politique et littéraire* (London) when commenting on the total inability of the costly school run by the Opéra to train singers: 'For the past ten years, it has not managed to produce a single one, for if a singer has appeared to distinguish herself in recent times, it is only to M. le Chevalier Gluck that we owe it.'[4] Piccinni appears to have been intimidated by the furore into abdicating any leadership role. In Italy, the composer customarily led his new opera himself from the harpsichord. Paris, however, had two different factors. Italian opera needed only a handful of soloists, but French opera had an enormous cast of soloists, chorus, and dancers. Second, the hostility from elements among the singers and orchestra, as well as the press, could scarcely have failed to have a chilling effect on one who had not been given a warm welcome.

According to the *Correspondance littéraire*, Marmontel's anger burst out one day when understudies were again to be used for rehearsing *Roland*. He declared harshly that he would not tolerate his friend's opera being performed by understudies and tore the music from the hands of the young man who was to replace Joseph Le Gros.[5] Recall that Gluck had been able to stipulate that no understudies be used and that another opera had to be ready should any singer be unable to perform. Marmontel's action, of course, alienated the singers. His anger is understandable, for these understudies were incompetent, but it is unfortunate that he did not recognize the manipulation of those who knew his weaknesses.

Singers wielded considerable power. Back on 5 September 1777, the *Courier politique et littéraire* reported that the implacable attitude of some had played a role in the downfall of Sacchini's *Olympiade* (see p.87), with one of them insisting: 'There is only one truth in music and M. Gluck has found it.'[6] This singer was later identified as Henri Larrivée who was to sing the title role in Piccinni's *Roland*. On 2 December 1777, the *Courier* observed:

> It is hoped that M. Piccinni's *Roland* will appear in January, if all the difficulties met with at this theatre allow it to be prepared. Already the principal singer (the one who caused *Olympiade*'s rejection and said that there is only one truth and M. Gluck has found it) finds his dignity compromised by going to Maestro Piccinni's. He demands that he [Piccinni] come to his place, on his knees apparently to implore mercy.[7]

Shortly after *Roland*'s first performance, the *JP* (5 February 1778) printed a letter from Larrivée repeating the same sentence about Gluck quoted above.

Before *Roland* opened, Piccinni believed his ruin was inevitable and sent Ginguené a letter announcing his intention to leave Paris. The day of the premiere, the composer's family was too frightened to attend and implored him to stay home. Amid tears and tumult, he remained calm and firm in his resolve to attend his opera. To everyone's surprise, *Roland* had a striking success and Piccinni was brought home in triumph. 'Despite the clamour of some men of party', says Ginguené, '*Roland* only succeeded more with each performance'.[8] The *Correspondance littéraire* concurs in this judgment:

> By dint of patience, sorrows, and prayers, this opera succeeded in being performed, and performed so well that, despite all the cabals and

[partisans of] the new and old music, never was a new opera followed with more eagerness. The Gluckist party persists in maintaining that it is charming concert music and nothing more; that it tickles the ear, but certainly does not touch the soul; that it is made to please, but will never excite this enthusiasm, these ardent transports that the sublime melody of *Alceste* and *Orphée* makes them feel ... Mlle Rosalie Levasseur performed the role of Angélique ably enough, but her inflexible voice is not at all suited to Piccini's music the way it is to Chevalier Gluck's. M. Larrivée surpassed himself in the role of Roland, especially in the superb monologue of the third act: 'Ah! j'attendrai longtemps, la nuit est loin encore.' It is the piece that seemed to make the most effect. To console themselves, *messieurs les Gluckistes* assure us that this piece is purely French.[9]

In a further commentary about the inflexibility and heaviness of voices at the Opéra, the *Correspondance littéraire* noted in April 1778 that Mlle La Guerre had replaced Mlle Levasseur in *Roland*:

> If she has fewer graces in her singing, she has a voice infinitely sweeter and more flexible; she grasps more soundly the expression and style of this song whose divine melody our French ears have so long disdained, but to which they finally seem more sensitive.[10]

The *Courier politique*, too, had earlier made a similar observation:

> Mlle Levasseur, who at the last performances of *Armide* [by Gluck] attained a height so difficult to attain, is miscast in the role of Angélique; her severe and loud [*seche & bruyante*] voice is not at all suited to the accents of love.[11]

This contrast in vocal quality is useful for understanding the type of powerful voice that was considered appropriate for Gluck's operas. The *Courier* also noted *Roland*'s success:

> Those who believed that the first performance would be chaotic would have been very surprised. Never has an opera been heard more attentively and never have the musical beauties worthy of notice been more unanimously and strongly applauded than on this day.[12]

After a year of attacks by the *JP* on those who wanted Italian music to be heard, there may have been a backlash. The constant torrent of mockery must have created a desire to see what all the fuss was about. In contrast to the massive coverage the *JP* offered Gluck's works, even when they had been playing for some time, it gave the opening of *Roland* only the customary perfunctory listings. The review of the first performance is short, much shorter than its reviews of other works whose composers remain obscure, and consists primarily of praise for the singers and dancers. After a few days, Marmontel's libretto was criticized, and on 8 February, an anonymous letter attacked La Harpe with a mocking account of the *Roland* review in his journal.[13] But he had learned the lesson that response would be futile.

The connoisseurs' favourable opinion about Piccinni's next opera (*Atys*), says Ginguené, was not shared by the very strong, active party ranged against him in the public, in the journals, and especially in the orchestra and among the singers. The first performance on 22 February 1780 was executed in a mediocre manner and coldly received. Moreover, noise from the standees on the *parterre* covered the instruments and voices. Subsequent performances were better, he adds, but this beautiful work did not have true success until revived years later.[14] Nevertheless, the *Correspondance litteraire* reacted favourably to *Atys*:

> The Gluckists themselves can scarcely avoid agreeing [about the value of *Atys*]. But this admission so painful does not prevent them from concluding that *Atys* is not a tragedy, that it is not even a beautiful opera. There are doubtless a multitude of beautiful airs, which would give the greatest pleasure in a concert, but they certainly do not comprise this admirable ensemble whose secret Chevalier Gluck alone knows. If it has to be admitted that *Atys*'s choruses are more highly finished than those of *Roland*, one takes revenge on the recitative, which is judged to be below Lully's because it is not in fact what it should be—a declamation supported by the simplest chords—or on the dance airs where one finds still less attention and variety than in those of *Amadis* [Lully]; etc. That's the spirit, *messieurs*; say as you will that *Atys* is only a beautiful concert, that the primary purpose of music is to move one and that this opera, which never screams, touches you only weakly. Speaking for myself, who seeks at the Opéra only the illusion of a sweet enchantment and the charm of a melody that is always pure and fresh, I beg that you permit me not to miss a single representation of *Atys*, if possible, and I will not refuse Mr. Gluck the only glory of which he seems jealous.[15]

The Mélophile

On 12 February 1778, the *JP* reviewed a programme by the elite Concert des Amateurs, in which a duet from Piccinni's *Roland* was performed:

> We cannot speak of this concert without mentioning the success of the duet from *Roland*, which had to be repeated twice. It is certain that

one cannot compare the effect of this duet at the Opéra with what it produced in concert.[16]

After asking if this generally made observation could not be regarded as proof of what some 'enlightened individuals' have put forward—that M. Piccinni's music is made for concerts or Italian opera—the writer continues:

> The true partisans of M. Piccini, those who without the blind partiality of a fanatic enthusiasm judge this celebrated artist with the greatest admiration, think that, in refusing him a great talent for dramatic music, one does no more harm to his reputation as a man of genius than one harms the reputation of Boileau and J[ean-]B[aptiste] Rousseau in refusing them the talents of Corneille and Racine, or in refusing La Fontaine the talents of Crébillon and M. de Voltaire.[17]

When performed in concert or at the Comédie-Italienne, Piccinni's music posed no threat to Gluck's supremacy at the Opéra. Although the *JP* rarely published opposing views, on 15 February 1778, it did include a letter from the Mélophile, who observes that if it does not harm the composer to say that he has no great talent for dramatic music but is destined only for concert music and Italian opera, it at least indicates a desire to do so:

> I do not know who these claimed *true partisans* of M. Piccini are, those who have an idea *so untrue* of his talents, but I know well that the greatest number of his admirers, *without the blind partiality of a fanatic enthusiasm*, have a much different one, and I am honoured to be among their number.[18] [The italics are original, the first and last indicating quotations from the *JP*'s review.]

The Mélophile then challenged the belief that Piccinni's music is suitable only for concerts and the Italian theatre.

Today, the Mélophile has been identified as Ginguené—apparently on the basis of the attribution in the posthumous Fayolle edition (Paris, 1818) of Marmontel's *Polymnie*. But this was negated by Ginguené's own description of the Mélophile, which included the observation that this individual felt obliged to make a justified defence of Piccinni and that his brochure brought an end to the quarrel.[19] The brochure is the pamphlet *Mélophile à l'homme de lettres chargé de la rédaction des articles de l'opéra dans le Mercure de France* (Naples, Paris, 1783), a response to Suard's anonymous critique in the *Mercure* (22 February 1783) of Piccinni's *Atys*.[20]

By publishing the Mélophile's 1778 letter, the *JP* indicated that the writer was one whom the Gluckists dared not offend. The aristocrat Jean-Benjamin de Laborde, *premier valet de chambre* at court until the death of Louis XV and instrumental in bringing Piccinni to Paris, is a likely candidate. Because the court supported Gluck, Laborde would have had to publish pseudonymously.

Laborde's *Essai sur la musique ancienne et moderne* (1780) awarded Piccinni a laudatory biography of several pages, including an evaluation of the art developed in his works:

> richness of invention; a proper and wise use of musical science, never degenerating into affectation and pedantry; harmony that is pure, clear and at the same time profound; melody that is perfectly analogous to the subject and situation ...; and finally, strength, originality, and some resources heretofore unknown in every genre.[21]

Continuing, Laborde says that Piccinni won the approbation of all sensible people and all the connoisseurs in Paris:

> Despite so many ridiculous criticisms and fierce enemies, he created from a poem of little interest in a language he scarcely understood ... for a nation whose taste, nature, and theatrical system were absolutely unknown to him—he created, I say, an opera full of delightful pieces. Angélique's first cavatina, Médor's *récit*, the sublime duet and the air *Je renonce à ce que j'aime*. The airs *Non je ne cherche plus cette source terrible: c'est l'amour qui prend soin lui-même*; the beautiful scene with Roland, followed by the air *Tu sais ce que j'ai fait pour elle*; the duet of Roland and Angélique: the air of *L'aimable objet qui m'enchante*; the beautiful *Monologue*, and especially the frightening air *Que me veux-tu, monstre effroyable* will always be in every mouth, on every music desk, and heard with transport at the theatre as long as one will sing music in France with French words.[22]

The frontispiece to *Livre cinquième* of Laborde's *Essai sur la musique*, which is an engraving of Lully and Piccinni (Figure 6.1), implies that they are equals in the field of opera, though separated by a century.

On several occasions during the years preceding the publication of Laborde's *Essai sur la musique*, the *JP* published substantial articles about his project and its subscription list, clearly expecting him to furnish a glowing endorsement of Gluck in his *Essai*. Hence the *JP* expressed disappointment when his book gave Gluck's works only brief mention. Laborde's high standing in society enabled him to reply:

Figure 6.1 J.-B. de Laborde. Frontispiece of *Essai sur la musique*, vol. 3.

If I did not dwell more on the merit and works of the celebrated Gluck, it is because the extraordinary sensation this composer produced is such that one is almost generally either his enthusiast or his detractor. Consequently, my judgment, whatever it had been, could not fail to excite dissatisfaction, and I felt it best to abstain. Moreover, the simple listing of M. Gluck's works itself is praise for him because of the striking success they call to mind.

The reputation he has among true connoisseurs would be still greater if some intolerant and prejudiced partisans did not diminish the number of his admirers by wanting to augment them by force. M. Gluck does not need to be extolled; it is sufficient that he be heard.[23]

Laborde was in a position to exercise independence that would be unthinkable to a musician whose livelihood might depend on favourable treatment by the *JP*. He seems the most likely candidate to have been the Mélophile, as Ginguené was then too insignificant to warrant the *JP*'s notice.

Journalists under siege

Although divisive events continued on a smaller scale for several years, Marmontel and La Harpe refused to participate. On 28 March 1779, La Harpe advised a M. Lamin:

> I am not at all surprised that the editors of the *Journal de Paris* have refused your letter. Would you want Satan, as the Evangelist says, to war against himself? I would be very pleased to enrich my journal [now

the *Mercure*] with it, but allow me to say that this would be to renew the war, an interminable war against invisible enemies who exist only to war. Do you not see that it is a snare set for us, and that the *Journal de Paris*, if it does not have the resource of some quarrel, is reduced to sustaining its authors, like its readers, with chaff.[24]

From the *JP*'s inception, the quarrel was a snare set for non-Gluckists, with nearly all the cards on one side. Against the torrent of anonymous writing on Gluck's behalf in 1777, the Piccinnists' writing comprised primarily the few items from Marmontel and La Harpe discussed above.

The *JP*'s intent to intimidate other journalists made La Harpe a tempting target. On 5 August 1776, some months before the *JP* began publication, he became editor of the *Journal de politique et de littérature* (*JPL*), already troubled by discord. According to the *Dictionnaire des journaux 1600–1789* (1991): 'A campaign of defamation was then thrown against the celebrated critic.' Recall that during 1777, the *JP* published not only all the music-related articles and anonymous letters against La Harpe described above, but also at least eight substantial articles about non-musical subjects in his journal. In 1778, the attacks increased greatly in frequency and length, so that several entire issues, aside from a few routine announcements, were devoted to this subject, weakening his journal to the point where the merger was the only solution.

On 6 June 1778, the *Correspondance secrète* wrote that Suard had designs on the *Mercure de France*, the flagship of French journals:

> It was believed that M. Suard would obtain the *Mercure's privilège*, but, lacking the funds and not wanting this morsel to escape him, he advised Panckoucke, his brother-in-law, to take it upon himself. Consequently, this publisher offered to pay all that the journal owed ... and he holds the *privilège*.[25]

In June 1778, the *JPL* was absorbed into a rejuvenated *Mercure*, whose *privilège* Charles-Joseph Panckoucke had just purchased, and La Harpe became its co-editor.[26] The new *Mercure* established a section for the political material previously in La Harpe's journal.

By silencing La Harpe with attacks designed to terminate his journal, the Gluckists sent a clear signal to other journalists, as noted in the *Entretiens sur l'état actuel de l'Opéra de Paris* (Amsterdam, 1779, p. 119) by Claude-Philbert Coquéau, an architect and published author who wrote independently in 1779:

> They [the Gluckists] have put all the journals on guard, even the one where M. de la Harpe had contended with them for a long time. They

have done so much that it is no longer permissible to speak aloud against M. Gluck or for M. Piccinni, and there are a thousand other underhanded maneuvers ... But it is more distressing than amusing for me to think that in such a matter where freedom should be complete, one wants to employ all the ruses of party spirit and all the transports of fanaticism and intolerance.[27]

Seeing in Coquéau's work a further opportunity for disinformation, the *JP* issued two anonymous letters, the first signed by 'Les Gluckists' on 4 July: 'The author of this brochure, in assuming to criticize the works of M. le Chevalier Gluck in an extravagant and ridiculous manner, and to lavish praises still more extravagant and more ridiculous on the music of *Roland* [etc.].' This was followed up on 7 July with a fabricated letter purported to be from 'Les Piccinistes':

> Our admiration for M. Piccinni is not exclusive; in fact it extends to all the great Italian masters, old and new. Along with the rest of Europe, we believe that there is no other music than Italian, and that Piccinni is one of the most skillful composers Italy has ever had; that is all there is to it. With pleasure, we even praise what is good in M. Gluck's works; that is, whatever is closest to the Italian genre.[28]

With the best of intentions, Coquéau had furnished the *JP* more fodder.

Suard's new influence at the *Mercure* enabled him to issue a sharp rebuke to Coquéau: 14 and 13 pages in the second and last issues for July 1779. Coquéau submitted a response and corrected a proof, only to find that it had been mangled without his knowledge when published on 14 August. He then published a *Suite des Entretiens ... ou lettres à M. S**** with his original response, preceded by an *avertissement* explaining the circumstances.[29] When writing to the Russian court, La Harpe relates Coquéau's struggle to be heard, and alludes to the Gluckists' tactics against journalists:

> The cabal heads, who had seized power from all the journals in order to silence all who did not think as they or to deprive them of the means to be heard, have lost much of their influence. Their despotism has made them loathsome and their underhanded maneuvers have made them contemptible.[30]

Back in February 1778 the *Mercure* had given Piccinni's first Paris opera, *Roland*, a favourable review of two and a half pages, a fairly customary length, but Suard's presence at the *Mercure* in 1779 enabled him to promote Gluck's *Iphigénie in Tauride* with four articles of elaborate praise: 8 pp. on 25 May; 11 pp. on 5 June; 9 pp. on 15 June; 2 pp. on 10 July.

Discord fomented

In this campaign, the most inflammatory snare consisted of the many anonymous letters published in the *JP*, which the *Correspondance secrète* attributed to Suard:

> M. S ... dedicates himself to Gluck's defense, and by an enthusiasm worthy of the greatest men, leaves the wings where he runs after the little actresses, steps on his friends, hastens to Vaugirard to put on the baker's apron, and there composes for us some letters that he sends into all the cafés, and which he will have end up miserably in the *Journal de Paris*. This is not a tale. M. de la Harpe, M. Marmontel and M. Suard were great friends. The quarrel of the Gluckists and Piccinnists happened unexpectedly. Despite his friends' advice, M. Suard wanted to write letters, and has been abandoned. Everyone has turned his back on him, but in compensation he has been named Adviser to the great Council of the Opéra, at a salary of 2000 *livres*.[31]

Suard apparently did not mind the loss of friends, which suggests that the monetary and other rewards were substantial. With respect to Arnaud, however, there was a history of long-standing enmity with Marmontel.[32] As stated above, La Harpe had earlier considered Suard a friend. In his *Polymnie*, Marmontel indicated the same when Suard (in the person of Finon) says:

'—Pour celui-ci, dit Finon, je l'estime;	'—Now this one, said Finon, I esteem him;
'Il fut vingt ans mon plus fidèle ami,	'For 20 years he was my most faithful friend,
'Jamais son coeur ne se livre à demi.	'Never yielded his heart to doing things halfway;
'Et j'en étais dépositaire intime:	'And I was an intimate depository of it:
'Je sais donc bien comme on peut le blesser;'[33]	'I thus know very well how he can be wounded.'

For many years, Marmontel had trusted Suard and assisted him in his career, which gave Suard an opportunity to see his vulnerabilities. The anonymous letters in the *JP* are filled with obscure references that mean little to us until explained in another source.

The cafés, too, served to disseminate discord. In his *Mémoires ... sur Suard* (1829), Dominique Joseph Garat related that Suard's *Anonyme* letters attracted throngs:

> People ran from everywhere to the Café de Foi et du Caveau, where there were public readings. To hear better, they squeezed together, suffocating themselves. With enthusiasm and bravos, they clapped hands to applaud Gluck and his music.[34]

In 1778, Marmontel wrote that Piccinni's *Roland* achieved great success, despite the efforts of the most indecent cabal and the attempts to disparage it in the cafés and papers six months in advance.[35] A good deal of communication was oral. Emotions fanned by the anonymous letters in the *JP* could be raised to an even higher pitch by verbal insinuations and offhand remarks. In an epigram, Marmontel related the reaction of an old supporter of Jean-Baptiste Lully (d. 1687):

Suard un jour débitant au Caveau	Suard, reciting at the Caveau one day
Ce qu'en trois mois il apprit de musique,	What in three months he had learned of music,
Prêchait sur Gluck, et sur le sens nouveau	Preached about Gluck and the new sense
Qu'avait créé l'Amphion germanique.	The German Amphion had created.
On l'écoutait: tout seul à son écot,	They listened to him; all alone in his reckoning,
Un vieux Lulliste, outré d'impatience	An old Lullist, incensed with impatience
De son babil: Quel est, dit'il tout haut,	At his babble, said loudly: Who is
Ce discoureur plus ennuyeux qu'un sot,	This talker more boring than a blockhead,
Qui déraisonne avec tant d'importance?	Who speaks nonsense with so much importance?
—Lui, c'est Suard, le confrère d'Arnaud.	—It is Suard, Arnaud's colleague.
Au Louvre assis, muet par prud'hommie,	Seated at the Louvre, silent by *prud'hommie*,[36]
Il n'y fait rien, et n'y dit jamais mot.	He does nothing, and says not a word.
—Eh! Que n'est-il, puisque tel est son lot,	—Since such is his portion, why is he not
Muet ici comme à l'Académie?[37]	Silent here as at the Académie Française?

According to the *Correspondance littéraire* (April 1779), La Harpe endured further insults:

> M. de La Harpe has just published a collection of his principal works in six volumes. It is immediately after the deplorable end of the

Barmécides [La Harpe's play], at the moment when M. de La Harpe has seen himself most cruelly tormented by his numerous enemies, and especially by the powerful sect of the Gluckists, that this new collection of his works has been offered to the malignity of the public and hatred of the journals. He has not been rendered all the justice that he would perhaps have obtained under different circumstances.[38]

The club of Hercules

'Your musical (or anti-musical) brochures tell me that the Teuton is armed with the club of Hercules,' declared Ferdinando Galiani to Marmontel on 30 November 1777.[39] And so it seemed. Playing a significant role in Gluck's success was Queen Marie Antoinette, who attended his operas frequently and made her admiration apparent to all. At the premiere of *Iphigénie en Aulide* on 19 April 1774, the *Mémoires secrets* reported on (the then Dauphine) Marie Antoinette's reaction:

> The Chevalier Gluck did not have as complete a success as his supporters had predicted. The greater part of the applause lavished on him could well be attributed to the audience's desire to please the Dauphine. This princess seemed to have manipulated the acclaim, and would not stop applauding, which obliged the Countess de Provence, the princes, and all those in the boxes to do the same.[40]

But when Piccinni's *Roland* opened in 1778, the *Mémoires secrets* reported that the young queen did not applaud: 'One knows how she protects Chevalier Gluck and loves his music.'[41] In January 1775, the *Correspondance littéraire* recounted a song inserted during a performance of Gluck's *Iphigénie en Aulide*:

> Chantons, chantons notre reine, Let us sing to our queen,
> Et que l'Hymen qui l'enchaine And may the wedlock that binds her
> Nous rende à jamais heureux. Make us forever happy.

> The piece was repeated, and all eyes turned toward the queen, who received this homage with the most pleasing and captivating embarrassment. What prologues, what panegyrics can be compared to these transports of tenderness and public admiration![42]

The *JP* always took special care to give singers, whose attitudes could influence the success of a work, the same accolades it gave Gluck, singling out some for particular attention. On 10 January 1778, shortly before Piccinni's *Roland* was to open, the *JP*'s front page was dedicated to a poem flattering

Rosalie Levasseur, Gluck's leading singer. In contrast, Ginguené reported having heard Gluck say after the performance of his *Armide*: 'The French make me laugh. They want song made for them and they don't know how to sing.'[43] According to Galiani in Naples, Piccinni told him about hearing Gluck make a similar remark at a dinner to honour the two composers.[44] The faulty French vocal method is deplored in so many sources, both domestic and foreign, that Gluck's comment is entirely plausible.[45]

Another instance of political power began with a conciliatory letter in the *JP* (6 June 1778) from Anne-Pierre-Jacques Devismes, the new director of the Paris Opéra:

> The debut of the *Opéras Bouffe* [a reference to Italian opera] is going to decide this great question debated so long by our most capable *Amateurs* [upper-class individuals]: 'Should Italian music be admitted to our theatre or be relegated to concerts?' Many people claim that this new and bizarre genre *is going to harm the majesty of the Opéra*. This fatal maxim has been an insurmountable barrier up to this moment. We are venturing to cross it, and if the public seems content with our efforts, it will then be easy to extend and vary to infinity the succession of its pleasures. The treasures of Jommelli, Galuppi, Majo, Traetta, Sacchini, Piccinni, Paisiello, and Anfossi will be open to us; it is only a matter of making a choice that is favourable and suited to the taste of our spectators.[46]

Devismes proposed to Gluck the idea of both composers writing an opera based on Euripides' *Iphigenia in Tauris*. Although Gluck had claimed to have burned his work on *Roland* when he heard that Piccinni was working on it, he now accepted this challenge and was given a good libretto by Nicolas-François Guillard. Du Roullet's letter of 15 May 1778 to Franz Kruthoffer, secretary to the Imperial ambassador, reveals that Gluck's *Iphigénie en Tauride* was well underway before Devismes's letter to the *JP*:

> [Gluck] has asked for changes to *Iphigénie*; I am sending them to you so that you might have the goodness to forward them to him by the first courier. There is no time to lose, for he [Devismes?] has given the queen his word to produce an opera before her confinement. *Iphigénie* must be ready for the month of November.[47]

After Gluck had departed Paris around February 1778, Devismes told Piccinni that he wanted to provide a magnificent occasion to showcase his talents. He assured him of the libretto's excellence and promised that his opera would be the first performed. To produce the effect that he anticipated from this new competition, he insisted on secrecy.[48]

Gluck wanted a higher fee for *Iphigénie*, but Kruthoffer's letter to Gluck (4 September 1778) urges him to accept Devismes's offer, adding that his Excellency 'hopes to secure for you, if not the whole sum you have asked for, at least that of 12,000 *livres*'.[49] Gluck declined coming immediately but apparently was then able to drive a hard bargain with Devismes.[50] On 1 November, Gluck wrote to Kruthoffer that he plans to be in Paris by 20 November 1778.[51]

Meanwhile, Piccinni had been working on his *Iphigénie* in total secrecy, complying with Devismes's stipulation. When to his surprise he learned that Gluck was about to present his *Iphigénie* at the Opéra, he informed Ginguené about the circumstances of his own *Iphigénie*, noting that he had reminded the director (Devismes) about his promise to produce his opera first, but the director replied that it was by order of the queen and he had no other choice. After examining the libretto by Alphonse du Congé Dubreuil given to Piccinni, Ginguené insisted on revisions.[52]

The Opéra produced Gluck's *Iphigénie en Tauride* in May 1779 and Piccinni's in January 1781. Before the latter's first performance, Piccinni wrote to the *JP*, expressing his concerns. On 22 January, the day after Piccinni's *Iphigénie en Tauride* opened, the *JP* published his letter, which observes that in Italy the same libretto is set by different composers without producing parties, quarrels, or comparisons. Because what is established in Italy by the most habitual usage is singular in France, he wishes to explain the circumstances. While working on the future *Atys*, he was given a libretto for *Iphigénie en Tauride*. He was aware that M. Gluck had departed for Vienna with an opera on the same subject. Knowing all the unpleasant occurrences and risks of rivalry, and careful to avoid all that could revive the quarrels, he refused this libretto in the most definite terms. Sometime later, they approached him again, giving convincing proof that Gluck had given up the project of returning to Paris. Piccinni was without work (implying income), and they pressed him to fulfil his engagement. No longer could he think about the libretto for *Atys*. He submitted reluctantly and set to work on *Iphigénie*. He had finished some acts when Gluck arrived in the most unexpected manner and gave his *Iphigénie en Tauride*. At least for the moment, Piccinni had to abandon the completed acts and any hope for seeing them produced. If this misfortune had attacked only his reputation, it would not have mattered so much. But as the father of a family and obliged to support them by the fruits of his labour, it was painful to see six months of work lost for his children and himself. Now that nearly two years have passed since Gluck gave his *Iphigénie*, Piccinni observes that his own could not harm Gluck's interests or reputation. The success of his work was decided a long time ago, and Piccinni neither can nor wants to destroy it. He then describes the considerable difference between the two librettos, so that no comparison can be drawn between the individual pieces in the two works. In its response to this letter two days later, the *JP* adopted a more moderate tone than usual, restricting its remarks to a commentary about the Italian practice of multiple operas on the same libretto and a comparison of the significant differences between the two *Iphigénie* librettos. Nothing was said about the composition itself, except to note the pieces that were well received.[53] With respect to this production, the *Correspondance littéraire* reported:

> It is time to say a word about this music that to us seems ready to disarm envy, prejudice, criticism and even the Gluckists. It is impossible to imagine a melody more sensitive and touching than that of all the airs in Iphigénie's role. The power of song has perhaps never been taken further than in the beautiful friendship scene in the third act, and especially in Pylade's divine air, *Oreste, au nom de la patrie*, and in the ravishing trio ending this act, which has the most completely dramatic and genuine expression. M. Piccinni was criticized for having neglected most of the choruses in *Roland* and *Atys*, but his *Iphigénie* has not one that is not of the greatest beauty. We cannot refrain also from recognizing in the recitative of this new opera much more movement, effect, warmth, and truth. What then does it lack for the greatest success? Some dance airs that are livelier or ballets more varied? Can one honestly believe this? One thing is clear: however acclaimed has been this celestial music, it attracts fewer people than *Le Seigneur bienfaisant* [by Étienne Joseph Floquet], which is having its fourteenth or fifteenth representation. After this proof, how can one still doubt if we in France have eyes or ears?[54]

According to Ginguené, Piccinni's *Iphigénie* succeeded beyond expectations, despite the handicaps of a libretto much inferior to the one given Gluck, a very active cabal, and some public bias in favour of Gluck's already performed *Iphigénie*. Although the second performance was marred by the leading lady appearing on stage in an intoxicated condition, the opera had 20 successive performances and would have had more if it had not suddenly and without reason been withdrawn, even though the receipts had not at all yet fallen below 3,000 *livres*. It is one of those injustices that we find more implausible, he added, the more distant the time when it occurred.[55] Because the only daily paper was in the hands of the Gluckists and had overwhelming power to influence events and public opinion, the length of an opera's run and its receipts prove little about its merit.[56]

By controlling the Opéra administration, the crown, the singers, and the only daily paper, as well as most of the other journals that had been cowed into submission, the Gluckists held the club of Hercules and possessed the might described by Nietzsche. Besides Suard and Arnaud, someone behind the scenes must have orchestrated these events. Above, the *Correspondance littéraire* referred to Du Roullet's 'impertinence', which might provide a clue in this regard.

Notes

1 Ginguené, 35f.
2 Ibid., 36–38.
3 *CL* (February 1778), 12:58f.
4 *CPL* (27 June 1777), 91.
5 *CL* (February 1778), 59.
6 *CPL* (5 September 1777), 256.
7 Ibid. (2 December 1777), 456.
8 Ginguené, 37f.
9 *CL* (February 1778), 12:59f.
10 *CL* (April 1778), 12:85f.
11 *CPL* (3 February 1778), 84.
12 Ibid.
13 On 25 April, the *JP* published another anonymous letter ridiculing a letter in La Harpe's journal. See [Leblond], 412, 420.
14 Ginguené, *EMM*, 1:627.
15 *CL*, 12:377f.
16 *JP* (12 February 1778), 171.
17 Ibid.
18 *JP* (15 February 1778), 182.
19 Ginguené, 62f.
20 *QGP*, 2:595–621.
21 Laborde, 3:220f.
22 Ibid.
23 Laborde letter, *JP* (8 May 1780), 531.
24 La Harpe-2, 35.
25 *CS*, 6:271.
26 Rémy Landy, *DJ*, 628f.
27 Coquéau, *QGP*, 2:485.
28 [Leblond], 463–66. Trans. adapted from Darlow, 183.
29 Online at Gallica.org. The *CL* (12:305) calls this essay 'infinitely better written' than his first one. It contains some 'very sound observations about the principles of the art, about *l'esprit*, about *vivacité*, about taste, together with excellent logic'.
30 La Harpe-1, 3:27f.
31 *CS* 10:68f. Cited by Kaplan, 116.
32 Kaplan, 26–28.
33 Kaplan, 25, 120. My translation.
34 Garat, 2:252. Cited by Kaplan, 116.

35 Marmontel, *MF* (15 September 1778), 179f. Cited by Kaplan, 116.
36 *Prud'homme*: member of a board of arbitration between employers and workers.
37 Quoted by Kaplan, 118n. from La Harpe, *Oeuvres*, 11:247f. (my translation).
38 *CL*, 12:246–48.
39 In Marmontel-4, 1:318.
40 *MS*, 7:162f. Trans. Howard, 113f.
41 *MS*, 11:78.
42 *CL*, 11:12.
43 P.-L. Ginguené, 'France', in *EMM*, 1:628.
44 Cited by Howard, 182f.
45 Vauthier, 294.
46 *JP* (6 June 1778), 627. Here, the name is given as 'Anne-Pierre-Jacques de Vismes de Valgay'.
47 Howard, 187.
48 Ginguené, 47–49. Howard, 197.
49 Howard, 193.
50 Ibid., 195.
51 Ibid., 195f. Asow, 140, 161.
52 Ginguené, 47–50.
53 *JP* (22 and 24 January 1781), 89f. and 96f.
54 *CL*, 12:473.
55 Ginguené, 52, 54.
56 *NG*, 'Piccinni', 709: 'Only when juxtaposed with a revival of Gluck's work was its [Piccinni's] undoubted inferiority to that masterpiece demonstrated, albeit crudely, by lower receipts.'

7 Disinterested observers

Is our perception of music from the past influenced by the manner in which it was received by contemporaries? And does this perception lead to underrating other composers' work, which did not have the benefit of extraordinary publicity? Three disinterested individuals from the period—two foreign and the third a Parisian of the next generation—offer pertinent observations about the Gluck/Piccinni controversy.

Johann Nicolaus Forkel

Although most foreigners steered clear of the Paris quarrel, in 1789, the future Bach biographer Johann Nicolaus Forkel used Du Roullet's 1772 letter published in the *Mercure de France*, which offered his and Gluck's work to the Paris Opéra (see p.13), to illustrate the deception employed.[1] Forkel also raised the question of whether music composition deliberately eschewing melody almost throughout in favour of declamation (recitative) is a valid musical form—the chief criticism from La Harpe and Marmontel about Gluck's music. To our ears, which are accustomed to such declamation in later operas, it is perfectly satisfactory, owing to the skill of today's singers. But, as seen in previous chapters, Gluck's music did not have the benefit of such vocal expertise during his lifetime. Therefore, an opera lacking recognizable melody was at a disadvantage. This is the context in which to view Forkel's concern. Most of his article is a translation of Du Roullet's letter, which, he said,

> should give the impartial friend of music some idea about the type of machine established for Gluck's *Iphigénie in Aulis* to obtain a reputation that it never would have been able to earn through its own intrinsic merit. The enlightened French were of this very opinion and remain so. But things were in France as in Germany: their voices

were shouted down by the crowd ... It is said that great musical masterpieces will last as long as great music endures. But who can say this of Gluck's music, which is not founded on natural art, but only on a type of musical declamation ... On the whole, the public has already decided all of this. As much as Gluck's music is discussed, it is seldom sung and played—not because it is too difficult or lofty to be used by many, but because it can too little be called music ... On the other hand, consider the *Walder* and *Romeo und Julie* by Georg Benda. Why are these sung, played and heard with delight by everyone? Because they contain true music, song, and expression of our feelings; not merely declamation, which, however, is part of it. Here we need no machines or praises in all the public papers; this music needs only to be heard to capture the hearts of both experts and music lovers. No war over it was necessary; its greater worth was at once universally and unanimously felt and recognized. With the former, on the contrary, attention had to be excited by exaggerated boasting, even by actual falsehoods ... It is certainly very useful for the art to expose such machines—which generally ... are planned only to lead the art's impartial friends, to their great **disservice**, away from the true way of Nature and confuse their eyes and ears.[2]

Forkel preceded Du Roullet's letter with his own imaginary cover letter to the *Mercure*:

> Despite the imprecations levelled against the [French] language of Racine, which is held to be unmusical, Paris is swarming with foreign composers who want nothing more than to dedicate their talent to our theatre. ... But, you ask, are they fluent with our language?—A much more important question would be: Do they also have genius? If this question is decided to their advantage, the other need not concern us.*
>
> > * If this is correct, as it in fact appears to be, it follows that the new type of opera, in which everything is founded upon declamation and only a little on the genuine art of music, cannot be a true musical form. Since it should be declaimed more than sung, composers must above all be skilled in language and correct declamation. But if genius is more important than language fluency, it contradicts everything that will be said below [in Du Roullet's letter]. That this is correct is shown by Handel, who understood little of the English language, but nevertheless composed masterworks in it. These, however, were song, not declamation.[3]

Now Forkel translates Du Roullet's letter, interspersing his own comments (indicated by an asterisk and set in italic type) in these two sample excerpts:

> the famous M. Glouch [sic], so well-known throughout Europe, has made a French opera that he would like to see produced on the Paris stage. After having composed more than forty Italian operas which have had the greatest success in all the theatres where this language is employed, this great man ...*
>
> *A count of **Gluck**'s operas can prove that they by no means amount to forty. Before coming to Paris, **Gluck**'s name did not appear in an Italian or other opera register. Hence it is impossible that his operas could have been performed in all the European theatres using the Italian language. ... At German courts, and particularly Dresden and Berlin where opera was so brilliant at the time of **Graun** and **Hasse**, one of his operas has never been performed. The previous king wanted to hear Gluck's Italian **Alceste** because so much had been said of it in Vienna. He put it to the test with his best singers and players, but after hearing some pieces, he had them stop because he was completely satiated. It was never produced.*[4]

Forkel is correct about Gluck's operas not totalling 40 in 1772, a number that could be approached only by including all the comic operas, one- and two-act pastorales, serenatas, and so forth. Many of the approximately 20 conventional three-act operas include heavy borrowing from earlier operas.

According to Du Roullet's letter, continues Forkel, Gluck's reform operas *Orfeo* and *Alceste* were produced in Parma, Milan, Naples, etc.: 'There they had an incredible success and produced a revolution in this particular art form in Italy.'*

> ***Gluck's** partisans have said and had it publicly printed that **his operas won the most extraordinary approbation in Florence and Venice** [boldface original]; the Italians affirm that one of his operas has never been performed in either Florence or Venice. It is further stated [by Gluck's partisans] that **fifteen years ago his opera Demophon was given in Milan, and is still today admired.** But after the most exacting inquiries to Milan, we have received assurance that he never composed an opera for Milan, and that merely his Orfeo was performed there.*[5]

Gluck's *Alceste* was not produced in Italy until several years after Du Roullet's letter (Padua, 1777; Naples, 1785; Florence, 1786). Although *Orfeo* subsequently became Gluck's most successful opera, at the time of

Du Roullet's letter, it had been performed only in Parma, 1769 (as part of a mixed spectacle for the wedding of Empress Maria Theresa's daughter); Bologna, 1771; and Florence, 1771 (where the empress's son Leopold was Grand Duke of Tuscany). The next Italian production was in Naples in 1774.[6] The 'Leblond' collection made a similar claim about *Orfeo* ('After having been performed twenty-eight successive times at Parma's theatre ...'), but it was performed just once for the aforementioned wedding.[7] As discussed above, the Italians customarily inserted arias by other composers into Gluck's operas to make them more acceptable to Italian taste. There is no record of a Gluck opera in Venice after his very early *Demetrio* (1742) and *Ipermestra* (1744). According to Forkel, Du Roullet further claimed:

> Last winter the city of Bologna produced one of those operas in M. Glouch's absence. His success there attracted more than 20,000 spectators who were eager to see the performance. From this production Bologna has earned more than 80,000 *ducats*, about 900,000 French *livres*.[8]

After finding no mention of this production in the Bologna papers for the normal opera season in 1771, Forkel concludes that it was a fabrication. *Orfeo*, however, was staged later that year in May and June for 27 performances as part of a production that also included Carlo Monza's *Aristo e Temira*. Nevertheless, Du Roullet's figure of its earnings was a fabrication, for it lost 10,000 *lire* for the impresario.[9] The number of seats sold, even if correct, does not indicate how many different people attended, for most of the boxes and many of the floor seats were purchased by the same individual for the entire season, when all social life centred around the theatre.

The exaggerations that Forkel cited are a sample of those subsequently used in Paris to promote Gluck's operas. With such a machine behind him, virtually every other able composer of the period could have achieved the same success.

François-Louis d'Escherny

Another non-Parisian offering useful commentary was the Swiss writer Count François-Louis d'Escherny (1733–1815), brother-in-law of Gluck's banker, Johann von Fries. Chamberlain to the king of Württemberg, d'Escherny was also an accomplished musician—a singer of good taste and a violinist able to hold his own in quartets.[10] His 1811 book includes a letter to his sister Anna von Fries from Gluck (16 November 1777; see Chapter 8), in which the composer comments on the controversy surrounding his operas and the large sums the new daily paper was earning for its publisher. D'Escherny's portrait of Gluck and his music differed from that of his Paris advocates:

> Gluck was a distinguished musician; above it was seen that I am pleased to do him justice. The operas he composed in Italy were not successful. Vocal music was not his talent; his arias and duets are a long way from the beauty, grace, and charm of those by Sarti, Hasse, Cimarosa, and Paesiello. Gluck had wits and he had to, for he was an adroit charlatan. By disdaining the Italian opera that revealed his lack of ability, he scorned the goal he could not attain. To smooth the road to Paris, he called it a bad genre, and praised French music. He also ventured to give the name of *fredon*, *gazouillement*, and *gargarisme* [pejorative terms for over-embellishment] to the heartfelt melodies composed and varied by great composers and virtuosos of the first rank.[11]

In 1767, d'Escherny had invited Gluck to a dinner that included M. Sevelinge, chairman of all the concerts. Although Gluck was at the time composing Italian opera, he praised Lully and French opera at great length, adding that he hoped to work for the Paris Opéra 'to draw from it true *tragédie lyrique*'. Upon returning to Paris, Sevelinge used his influence on Gluck's behalf. According to d'Escherny, Gluck's *airs* in his French operas imitate the sobriety and brevity of Lully's and resemble the recitative:

> In Lully, as in Gluck, we often do not know if what we hear is sung or recited. Gluck misjudged the use of music and abandoned its intended aim, which is to touch and move by means of melody and harmony ... His error was to give everything to the action [via declamation] and compete with French opera. He composed some operas that are neither musical nor of fine declamation; nor are they correct and well-written dramas; they are anomalies.
>
> Apart from some almost graceful fragments borrowed from Italy or France, his *airs* in general offer only broken-off and incomplete melodies. His operas lack what should predominate there—beautiful melodies, beautiful *airs*—and they are full of what they should lack—that is, his claimed declamation, which is nothing other than Italian recitative.[12]

D'Escherny credited Gluck with composing excellent music for Jean-Georges Noverre's ballets, as well as some beautiful overtures, such as the one from *Iphigénie*. But one will look in vain in all his operas for these beautiful arias and ravishing melodies performed by the great Italian castrati and first-rank female sopranos, nearly all of whom he had heard—from Farinelli to Marchesi, and from Hasse (Faustina) to Isabella Colbran and Josephina Grassini.[13] Observing that Gluck had composed *Orfeo* originally for Vienna and the title role for the castrato Gaetano Guadagni, fitting the music to his naturally sweet and touching but not agile voice, d'Escherny notes the advantage this gave the Vienna production over the one in Paris: 'Guadagni sang the role of Orfeo and did not scream it; [in Paris] Legros screamed it.' D'Escherny blames the Paris audience, whose enthusiastic applause encouraged screaming.[14]

Guadagni's gift for the title role helped assure *Orfeo*'s success in Vienna, but he had yet another talent. According to Jean-Benjamin de Laborde (1780), Guadagni composed all the music for his role in Ferdinando Bertoni's opera *Orfeo* given in Venice.[15] In a footnote, d'Escherny reported that Guadagni also composed certain parts of his role in Gluck's *Orfeo*:

> Above I said that Gluck's most beautiful melodies were not his, but I omitted a fact that I have from M. Ginguené, who is equally versed in literature and Italian music—that it is Guadagni himself who furnished Gluck most of the melodies for his role in *Orfeo*.[16]

In 1791, Ginguené judged *Orphée* (the French version of *Orfeo*) to be the best and purest of Gluck's works, although the melody in general, except for the title role, is inferior to Italian melody. If the style of Orphée's role is completely Italian, he added, it is because the melody of the first air '*Objet de mon amour*' ('*Piango il mio ben così*'), the three couplets that Orphée sings to appease the demons, and the charming rondeau in the third act are by Guadagni, for whom this role was created. Noting the difference between these truly Italian melodies and M. Gluck's other pieces, Ginguené considers Guadagni's contribution to be a well-known fact.[17] The 'three couplets' must refer to Act II/i: '*Laissez vous toucher par mes pleurs*'; '*Ah! la flamme qui me dévore*'; and '*La tendresse qui me presse*'. The rondeau in the third act is perhaps Gluck's most famous aria: '*J'ai perdu mon Euridice*' ('*Che farò senza Euridice?*' Ex. 7.1). The melodies of the French version follow their originals quite closely, although one of the couplets adds some florid measures. As a prolific, respected writer on a wide variety of subjects,

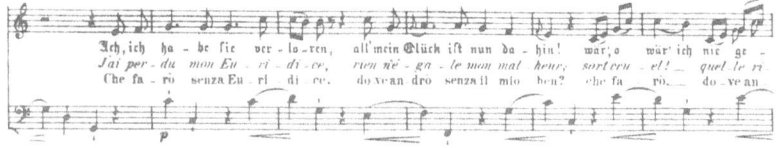

Ex. 7.1 Gluck, *Orphée*, 'J'ai perdu mon Euridice'.

Ginguené is unlikely to have been making an idle accusation of his own invention. If his statement is incorrect, there should be comparable melodic examples elsewhere in *Orfeo* or in Gluck's other operas. Inserting music by another hand into an opera was not unusual during this period.

Beautiful melodies and touching motives are the creation of genius, says d'Escherny, and nature withheld from Gluck the necessary inspiration. But nature granted him the talent for drawing from the harmony some grand effects of a sombre and dreadful type. This is what makes the underworld scene from *Orphée* excellent. His energetic and wild music for the devils is admirable; the contrast of Orphée's touching sounds with the infernal uproar of the demons is a very beautiful musical and dramatic conception.[18]

Of all Gluck's operas, *Orfeo* enjoyed the most success. Contributing factors include an appealing plot and libretto, Guadagni's stellar performance in the title role, more melody than customary in Gluck's reform operas, and the brevity of the whole production, which obviated the boredom of a form relying so heavily on declamation. Another element in its success, says d'Escherny, was external:

> With a charming appearance, Guadagni had the good fortune to touch the heart and turn the head of one of Vienna's most beautiful women. This woman of the highest social rank and still higher repute lent the opera her support from love of the singer; more would not have been necessary to carry it to the skies.[19]

Nevertheless, according to d'Escherny, the empress's protection was the primary factor in *Orfeo*'s success. Many of the subsequent performances took place in locations either under Habsburg domination or where a member of the royal family was present, as in Paris. Through marriage, Maria Theresa's progeny made advantageous affiliations in Bavaria, Saxony, the Netherlands, Parma, Spain, Naples, and France. More than half of *Orfeo*'s performances in some 20 cities and towns during the years from 1762 to 1782 can be identified as having Habsburg connections. That these associations could be very useful is shown by a letter from the future Joseph II to his brother Leopold, Grand Duke of Tuscany, on behalf of Antonio Salieri (who frequently deputized for Gluck) in early 1772:

> Gassmann's student, Salieri, the young man whom you know and whose music is so well-received, would like to find a theatre in Italy for which he could write an *opera buffa* or *seria* to become better known there. Would there be an opportunity in the spring for him to write something for Florence?[20]

Salieri's score accompanied this letter, and his *Locandiera* was performed in Florence in 1775.

Later opinion from Paris

In 1802, when the quarrel was but a memory, the theatre critic Julien-Louis Geoffroy reviewed a revival of Gluck's *Armide*, raising similar questions about the viability of a form that stresses declamation over melody:

> Quinault [the librettist] only weakened Tasso; the opera of *Armide* is languishing and prolix. To rekindle it would require celestial melody, not a declamation in notes. Only with difficulty did Gluck yield to this delicate and tender genre: he sometimes confused sweetness with monotony, voluptuousness with slowness. His bent for the bold and dreadful is in its place only in the fine chorus 'Poursuivons jusqu'au trépas' and in the act with *La Haine* [Hate, a character]. Gluck was excellent for making the lower regions speak and the devils sing. Nevertheless, he knew how to express tenderness when he wanted it; the duet 'Aimons-nous' is proof. Why did he not want it more often? Why is this duet the only moving piece in an opera that should express pleasure and love? This great composer, who could do everything he wanted, was too often misled by a false system of recitative and musical declamation, which distorts the true idiom of his art. He wanted … to reconcile melody with theatrical declamation. With this principle, neither music nor tragedy is produced, but only a great expenditure of harmony and talent to tire the listeners. A tragedy that is skillfully declaimed by excellent actors will always be more pleasing and interesting than the same tragedy set to recitative. Operas are and can be only an outline sketch that furnishes situations for music to express in its own language; this language is essentially different from declamation. Everything that is not song or an ensemble piece is thus only filler that the Italians have the good sense not to listen to. They alone know how to enjoy music; they savour the elixir of an opera and leave us to endure the dregs.[21]

This refers to the fact that Italian audiences almost never listened to simple recitative, but spent the time gossiping, playing cards, and visiting other boxes. In another review (1804), Geoffroy observed:

> Gluck knew that writing well was only half the battle for success. He sought a compromise that could adapt itself to French taste; he embellished and improved upon Rameau, and, above all, he had a predilection

for discrediting the Italian taste. He proclaimed the pretension of making conventional tragedies with music. He ostentatiously displayed the system always known in France as though it were new ... The greatest part of Gluck's glory is founded on his adroit regard for the old French music.[22]

Although Gluck essentially utilized the structure of the old French opera, his operas conveyed the illusion of innovation by achieving a higher level of execution.

Forkel, d'Escherny, and Geoffroy represent individuals of sound reputation who did not consider an opera based essentially on declamation to be a feasible and convincing musical form, thus confirming the Piccinnists' chief criticism of Gluck's music.

Notes

1 See Chapter 1, n. 30.
2 Forkel, vii–xi at x.
3 Ibid., 152n.
4 Ibid., 154n.
5 Ibid., 156.
6 *Orfeo* and *Alceste* dates: Alfred Loewenberg, *Annals of Opera* (Totowa, NJ: Rowman & Littlefield, 1978).
7 [Leblond], 474.
8 Forkel, 156.
9 Ricci, 491.
10 Pougin, 203f.
11 Escherny, 2:355f.
12 Ibid., 358ff.
13 Ibid., 361.
14 Ibid., 363.
15 Laborde, 3:317.
16 Escherny, 362n.
17 Ginguené, 'France', in *EMM*, 1:624.
18 Escherny, 365f.
19 Ibid., 363.
20 Braunbehrens, 59.
21 Geoffroy, 5:150f.
22 Ibid., 5:166f.

8 Profit and power

Further commentary from participants and observers will clarify some issues and provide a fuller picture of Gluck. At the same time, it raises questions.

The motives

In a letter (Paris, 16 November 1777) to his banker's wife Anna von Fries, François-Louis d'Escherny's sister, Gluck declares:

> To secure a great success for Piccinni's opera, the ambassador from Naples indefatigably intrigues against me, as much at court as among the nobility. He persuaded Marmontel, La Harpe, and several academicians to write against my system of music and my style of composition. The Abbé Arnaud, M. Suard, and some others undertook my defense, and the quarrel became so heated that insults would have led to deeds if mutual friends had not restored order among them. The *Journal de Paris* which is issued daily, is full of it. The quarrel is making a fortune for the editor, who already has more than 2,500 subscribers in Paris.[1]

Although Gluck blamed the Neapolitan ambassador, Domenico Carraccioli, for persuading Marmontel and La Harpe to write against him (omitting that they also saw much to praise in his work), it was his own inflammatory letters that prompted their writings. Shortly after Marmontel's article quoting Giovanni Battista Martini was published in the *Mercure de France* (1778; see Chapter 2), Gluck wrote from Vienna to Franz Kruthoffer in Paris (30 September 1778):

> I read your letter with great pleasure, but the *Mercure* annoyed me. Henceforth I have decided not to come to Paris until M. de Vismes succeeds in obtaining for me an assurance from the minister that the

law will not lay hands on me if I come to crop Marmontel's ears. As the *Journal de Paris* has not been able to make him humbler, he needs a more violent treatment, and this would be the best.²

Gluck had little to complain about. Not only did he have the crown's strong support, but also the *Journal de Paris* (*JP*) was praising him to the skies and promoting a divisive quarrel. The paper grew rapidly and, by 1779, required two printing shops to prepare a daily press run of 5,000–6,000 copies. According to Suard's biographer Dominique Joseph Garat (1821), the *JP* procured 100,000 *livres* for its owners from its first year.³ In contrast to the literary and political journals, whose profit margins were insignificant and readership small, the *JP* was a commercial enterprise.

Apart from financial considerations, there was the satisfaction of having a powerful instrument with which to settle old scores. While Marmontel and La Harpe were 'achievers', Suard and Arnaud were described by more than one contemporary as indolent. Their election to the Académie Française may have resulted from non-literary factors. After Arnaud's entry to this august body, the *Correspondance littéraire* (May 1771) included the 'Observations de M. Diderot', an unfavourable critique of Arnaud's discourse.⁴ Another article in this journal reports that people were asking:

> What has he produced? The *Journal étranger* and a literary gazette—which were not able to keep afloat as soon as the principal men of letters stopped contributing because the two associate editors, Abbé Arnaud and Suard, were too lazy, and attached to worldly pursuits and dining on the town to take the pains a periodical requires.⁵

Moreover, 'there was a time when the Abbé Arnaud wanted to make his fortune by calumniating the *philosophes*, and it is by no means certain today that he is among their friends'. Few took Arnaud and Suard to be serious scholars.

A further motivation for the *JP*'s type of journalism: A few men were now enjoying the unprecedented, heady power that formerly belonged only to the sovereign. The control over public opinion achieved by a daily paper with a monopoly far exceeds anything that a literary or political journal appearing at wide intervals could offer in response, even if it were free to express opinions. With some strokes of the pen, they were able to throw a large portion of the literate public into strife and contention. It must have been intoxicating.

It is difficult to imagine the animosities created by this quarrel, which was incited with such cunning that few knew its origin (see Chapter 3, Notes 10, 13, 14, 50). When the *Mémoires pour servir à l'histoire de la révolution opérée dans la musique par M. le chevalier Gluck* (the 'Leblond' collection of reprints) was published in 1781, tempers still ran high, as reported by the *Journal de littérature, des sciences & des arts*:

> The war, *Monsieur*, which for five or six years has divided the devotees of music, has not for an instant ceased inflaming the senses and producing antagonisms. Sometimes muffled and internal, it has not disappeared from societies and cafés; sometimes tumultuous and noisy, it manifests itself in the *parterres* [the male standees in the theatres] and the journals by violent explosions, and has given birth to cabals, brochures, failures and successes. Like political wars, this war has had varied events. Sometimes vanquished and sometimes triumphant, the two parties have made continual efforts to assure their victories or redeem their losses. Plans have been formed, snares set, assaults made, and, as in political wars, it has not necessarily been strength of reason or the combatants' worthiness that has overcome, but the number of cannons and men.[6]

Apart from Marmontel's *Essai sur les révolutions de la musique, en France* and La Harpe's few passages, this reviewer found no impartiality in the collection, unless it should be the place of publication—Naples. This, too, may be a witticism for their descendants: 'Who knows if some future scholar will use it to prove that M. Gluck's music was admired in eighteenth century Naples, but Paris alone still contested its beauty?'[7] Yes, the 'Leblond' collection seems to have influenced posterity. In his *Polymnie*, Marmontel describes this compilation of Gluckist writings (Finon represents Suard and Trigaud, Arnaud):

'-J'ai, dit Finon, rassemblé nos écrits;	'-I have, said Finon, assembled our writings;
'Ils ne font plus un volume si mince.	'A volume so thin doesn't suffice anymore.
'N'avons-nous pas les feuilles de Paris?	'Don't we have those of the *Journal de Paris*?
'Ce seul présent serait digne d'un prince.	'This gift alone would be worthy of a prince.
'Nous y donnons tous les jours du nouveau;	'Every day we offer something new there;
'C'est tour-à-tour mon génie ou le vôtre;	'By turns it's my genius or yours;
'J'ai donné l'ordre; on nous relie en veau,	'I've given the order for a binding in leather,
'Et nous serons accolés l'un à l'autre'	'And we will be bound one to the other.
'Trigaud surpris d'être enfin relié:	'Trigaud, surprised at being finally bound:
'Voilà, dit-il, un monument durable;	'Here, he says, a lasting monument;
'Quand on a fait cette oeuvre mémorable,	'When this memorable work is made,
'On ne craint plus de se voir oublié.'[8]	'We no longer fear being forgotten.'

According to Garat, Suard never avowed or disavowed writing the letters signed by the *Anonyme de Vaugirard*, despite their brilliant success. However modest Suard was, he had to have more than one reason to resist so continually the very natural temptation to put his name at the head of those of his works whose success had most resembled the acclamations of glory.[9]

Unlike Garat and most other supporters, however, Suard knew how posterity would eventually judge these works. Although his identity soon became apparent to those who knew him well, Garat implies that most people remained uninformed.

Garat claimed that Suard spoke of Marmontel's *Essai*, whether aloud or in his letters, only in terms of the highest esteem. He also maintained that Suard never missed an opportunity to praise La Harpe's taste and literary judgments. Remarkably, Garat painted a noble picture of Suard's character while condemning Arnaud's:

> Unfortunately, the Abbé Arnaud (who, without being at all courageous, was not at all reasonable either) shattered anew every day the *peace pipe* that M. Suard renewed each day. The Abbé did not pass all his life in turning and rolling Homeric periods into French prose. Without being defter than Boileau, he, too, made grand use of malice: he richly rhymed the Marotic epigram and made it very biting … Marmontel could not ignore the epigrams that all Paris recited. Madame Suard was very upset about it, and the Abbé laughed at his friend's affliction. M. Suard, who was not as affected as his wife but did not laugh like all Paris, vainly implored the Abbé to silence this sharpshooter fire, which does not win battles but degrades the most wonderful victories.[10]

Even if the epigrams can be assigned to Arnaud, authorship of the anonymous brief letters, most of which are just as offensive, remains uncertain. Their sharp decrease after Suard took a leave of absence in early 1778 may provide a clue. Although his long *Anonyme* letters seem to have a more elevated exterior tone, his techniques do not present a favourable view of his character. That Garat and others could consider them excellent testifies to a susceptibility to political rhetoric. Arnaud and Suard were spectacularly successful in their campaign of deception primarily because few disinterested persons then or now will take the trouble to check facts and the original text to see if it has been quoted accurately. Another possible author of short letters is Jean-Jacques Rousseau, who wrote the epigram against La Harpe in the *Lettre ... Par DAVID *** son Ami* (see p.70).

Writing after her husband's death, Amélie Suard, too, perceives Arnaud as the driving force in the controversy and seems unaware of her spouse's activities:

> The Abbé Arnaud, whose opinions were nearly always identified with those of M. Suard, so close was the friendship uniting them, was impassioned for Gluck, as he had earlier been for the Greeks. Usually full of good nature and politeness in literary discussions, he seemed to depart from his character of moderation when hearing such dramatic music by Gluck; his admiration for the German composer became exclusive. He was unjust toward Piccini and intolerant of all who did not bow at his idol's feet. He spoke of them only with the greatest scorn. He indulged in epigrams against Marmontel … 'Oh well', he said, 'we will have an *Orlando* and an *Orlandino*'. Marmontel was furious and shared his ill humour with Saint-Lambert and other mutual friends. And M. Suard, who had never been unjust toward Piccini, valued his talent, as can be seen in the *Anonyme de Vaugirard*'s letters. All of Abbé Arnaud's sentiments were attributed to M. Suard, who had to bear the pain of his exaggeration. Saint-Lambert and Mme d'Houdetot, then very close to Marmontel, received us in such a different manner than before that we stopped seeing them.[11]

From Mme Suard and Garat, can one infer that Suard did not have the strength of character to disassociate himself from Arnaud? Or were the financial rewards too great? Both Garat and Mme Suard indicated awareness that wrongs were committed against the Piccinnists. Judging from contemporary reports on both sides, Suard seems to have been a likeable man of charm with a gift for deception.

Yet there may be some truth in considering Arnaud the central commander of the Gluckists. His tenacious fanaticism is documented in his correspondence with Padre Martini. When he did not give Gluck the benefit of his hyperbolic praise, the composer's *Écho et Narcisse* (1779) failed. According to Marmontel's *Polymnie*, Gluck had imprudently ignored Arnaud's advice about choosing subjects from antiquity having a somewhat horrific tone.[12] The libretto for *Écho et Narcisse* offered no opportunity for the grand effects of volume and cries that had made Gluck's other operas so successful. In a letter of 29 December 1779, this opera's librettist Baron von Tschudi mentioned that Arnaud had 'abandoned' them.[13]

Much later, Suard's issue of his *Mélanges de littérature* (1803) gave the critic Julien-Louis Geoffroy occasion to muse that most of the articles in this collection are scenes. He found Arnaud dominant among the actors:

> The pieces he furnished for the collection are the least pleasing and useful. Abbé Arnaud ... made for himself an oriental jargon of which fine society was the dupe. He was one of the first to make fanaticism in the arts fashionable in Paris ... In mocking everything, he was a perfect egotist and one of the troupe's better charlatans. In the morning, he put on the cassock to ask M. d'Autun for a benefice; in the evening, clothed as a layman, he visited the boulevard's little theatres, of which he was a great devotee. By uttering nonsense about the Greeks, of which he had only a very superficial knowledge, he was received by the Académie des Belles-Lettres; his balderdash, which was taken for eloquence, opened the door of the Académie-Française for him. No one has characterized him better than Marmontel: *l'abbé Fatras* ['balderdash'] is an admirable brush stroke. This sobriquet is nearly the only fruit that the Abbé reaped from all his combats in favour of Gluck's music. This man who produced charming witticisms and was a pleasure to listen to in a circle is only a tedious babbler in his literary articles, which are full of words and empty of substance. Wit cannot replace erudition; one will always be inadequate on a subject one does not know.[14]

Although Geoffroy was not involved in the quarrel, which had taken place nearly a quarter century earlier, and was astonished that it engendered such bitter passions, he commented on it occasionally. In 1812, he reminisced about an event described in Chapter 6:

> To better compare and judge the two rivals, it was necessary to have them work on the same poem [*Iphigénie en Tauride*]; but care was taken to avoid this. Poor Piccini, who scarcely understood French, was given a pitiful work, and the good poem by M. Guillard was given to Gluck. The Italian was cruelly deceived: he had been deluded by the promise of having his opera performed before Gluck's, without which he would never have consented to engage in this competition— the one who appears first at the theatre has as much advantage as the one who plays first at *piquet*. But Piccini had completed only half of his work when he learned that Gluck's was going to be presented. He complained grievously, but it was alleged that it was by court order. Piccini was sweet, modest, peaceable, not at all an intriguer. He had all the aspects of talent, and talent was his only support. With such weak protection, it is strange that he did not become still more unsuccessful. Piccini knew how to create song and beautiful arias, but Gluck knew

the world and men; he knew how to turn the passions to account, a much more useful science.[15]

Gluck's financial acumen

Several accounts from the period portray Gluck as having more than a passing interest in money. In his *Mémoires*, Johann Christian von Mannlich, who served as artist in the household of Duke Christian IV where Gluck lived, tells of the duke's activities on the composer's behalf. Just after Gluck's first opera opened (April 1774), the duke recommended that a fair copy be prepared for the king. He himself would present Gluck to the sovereign, as Mannlich describes:

> The score of *Iphigénie* was bound in fine sky-blue satin, and my Lord the Duke took Gluck with him to Versailles. He was prepared for the occasion, and had donned a coat richly embroidered in gold. ... When strangers, even those of high rank, were presented to the king, he would pause for barely a moment in crossing the gallery on his way to Mass, and, without saying a word, acknowledge them with no more than a nod. But on this occasion, surrounded by all the court, he stopped to speak to M. Gluck. He accepted the score with pleasure, thanked Gluck, and complimented him on his opera's spectacular success. All the courtiers and many observers were astonished and asked who this extraordinary man was. Soon all Paris knew about this mark of high favour, and M. Gluck's real reputation rose a hundred percent in the Parisians' estimation. He was the only one not to feel its full value. Eventually, the duke, amazed at his protégé's silence, asked: 'Well, M. Gluck, are you pleased with the way you were received and welcomed by the king?' 'Yes, my Lord,' he replied, 'I was told that His Majesty very rarely spoke to those presented to him: I ought therefore to be very flattered to see him stop and talk to me, and receive my gift. But if I write another opera for Paris, I would rather dedicate it to a tax collector, because he would give me [ducats] instead of compliments.' This reply froze the assembled friends, who were all good courtiers, and visibly displeased the duke, who changed the subject.[16]

Some years later, the *Correspondance secrète* related another instance involving money. When the Opéra's directors wanted to bring Gluck back to Paris, they offered 6,000 *livres* as an annual salary independent of the proceeds from his compositions, the same arrangement as had been made with Piccinni:

> But the German knows his talents and is not a man to content himself pitifully with fame and praise. He loves money and it shows; his

final word was for 12,000 *livres* in fees plus the title: *Composer of the Académie de musique*. However exorbitant Chevalier Gluck's expectation appeared, the committee acquiesced. It was resolved that 9,000 *livres* would be taken from funds and that there would be a deputation to the queen to solicit from her munificence the other 3,000 *livres* necessary to attract to France a subject she loves, whose talents are precious to her. The queen generously supported this arrangement and promised to obtain the sum through the king's favour. Consequently, Chevalier Gluck's return is expected in a short while; this will be the third time, after having always promised that he would never return.[17]

Around 1779, the Opéra's new director Pierre Berton attempted to pacify the parties by reconciling the composers at a splendid dinner where they were seated together. Throughout the meal, they conversed with much cordiality. During dessert, Gluck, a little overheated by wine, pursued the path of candour and, in a manner to be heard by everyone, said:

> The French are good people, but they make me laugh. They want songs and do not know how to sing. My dear friend, you are a man celebrated in all of Europe. You think only of your art. You make beautiful music for them; are you better off for it? Believe me, making money is the issue here and nothing else.

Piccinni responded politely that Gluck's example proved that one could be concerned at the same time with both art and fortune. Afterwards, they parted very amicably and there was no doubt that their conduct was sincere. In Ginguené's words: 'They themselves were the two men who would have seemed to have the least party spirit.'[18] Nonetheless, the war of which they were the subject continued.

When the Berlin court Capellmeister Johann Friedrich Reichardt visited Vienna in 1783, he met with Gluck, who told him about his work in Paris. Gluck said he knew Paris and the Parisians through and through and spoke with irony about how he, in his own grand manner, had handled and taken advantage of them, in conformity with their stupidity and presumption.[19]

Summation

Although Gluck had held a near-monopoly at the Paris Opéra since 1774, the quarrel did not begin until the *Année littéraire* published Gluck's provocative letter in early 1777. This polarized public opinion and created for the first time what has been called the Piccinnist party. From its inception in January 1777, the *JP* published a steady stream of praise for Gluck while taunting Marmontel and La Harpe. In January, the *JP* began a series of provocations against Marmontel, whose response was limited to a scholarly *Essai* a few months later. Despite its tone of moderation, the *JP* attacked it many times with lies and mockery. Much later, Gluck's letter to the writer Charles Palissot de Montenoy (18 March 1780) showed that he still portrayed Marmontel as a bitter opponent:

> If, during my stay in Paris, I had known of your comedy *Les Philosophes* and your *Dunciade*, what good use could I have made of them against the invective of Marmontel and his party![20]

Had it not been for the composer's own inflammatory letter in the *Année littéraire*, Marmontel would probably never have written a word about Gluck's music. What he did write is well within the boundaries of acceptable criticism. In October 1777, Gluck played another pivotal role with his two letters against La Harpe (pp.82–83).

To what extent was Gluck involved in the quarrel and what was his proficiency with the French language? In his letter of October 1784 to the *Mercure de France*, Du Roullet referred to the composer's weakness with speaking the French language. On the other hand, his earlier letter in the *Mercure* (October 1772) claimed that Gluck knows Italian and French perfectly. Because French was spoken by the upper classes throughout much of Europe at this time, Gluck needed some fluency to work in the field of opera. He spent considerable time in Paris. In 1777, for example, he arrived on 29 May and did not leave until February 1778.

As noted on p.24, Arnaud's letter (1776) to Martini states that Gluck had put him in charge of the forthcoming *JP*. Then what was Gluck's relationship with the *JP*? Was he participating in its direction and reaping financial rewards? After de La Place's three-week tenure as director of the new paper, no director has been identified until 1785. Thus Arnaud, who died in 1784, could have been overseeing the operation anonymously. The *JP*'s massive *querelle* verbiage greatly lessened after 1777, perhaps because Suard took a long leave of absence in February 1778. The Piccinnists' refusal to respond to further attacks also played a role.

The Gluckists' continual provocation was a deliberate attempt to incite controversy, which served to stimulate interest in the new *JP* and secure its commercial success. Gluck's three closest associates in Paris—Arnaud, Suard, and Du Roullet—had no compunctions about violating conventional codes of behaviour in a campaign on his behalf. According to his letter above, he was aware that the quarrel was 'making a fortune' for the *JP*. It seems inconceivable that he was not rewarded handsomely. Gluck and his supporters also wished to retain his supremacy at the Paris Opéra and all that this entailed. Therefore, the Gluckists maintained that music in the

Italian style belonged only to concerts, not at the Opéra. Their misuse of the power and profit motive to attack innocent individuals in a vindictive manner explains the high passions aroused by the quarrel they incited. It was also an attack on the *philosophes*, their values, and accomplishments, as suggested by Suard's anonymous 1783 renewal of issues in the *Mercure*, long after the *JP* had obtained financial security.

The Piccinnists' struggle to admit any deserving work to the Paris Opéra eventually led to Paris becoming a leading European centre in the nineteenth century, but the way was long and opposition strong. After Piccinni's *Roland*, it became acceptable for the Opéra to stage Italian works. Progress continued with the appointment of François-Joseph Gossec as director of the new École Royale de Chant, de Déclamation et de Danse in 1784 with Piccinni in charge of the vocal department.

Since Marmontel's non-musical works have had many editions, it seems unusual that the useful information in his *Essai* has received so little attention. Have the ridicule and lies in the 'Leblond' collection of *JP* writings contributed to this neglect? Gluck's music is widely performed today, but not Piccinni's—justifiably, or as a result of the Gluckist campaign of deception? While the *New Grove Dictionary of Music and Musicians* (2001) awards Gluck an article of 36 pages, it grants Piccinni 7 pages. Gluck's works have been published in a collected-works edition of some 47 items, but a similar project for Piccinni's has not been undertaken. The events depicted above testify to the power wielded by money and an unbridled journalistic monopoly. In view of this and the fact that Piccinni's operas were highly regarded in Italy and much of Europe, a reappraisal would be appropriate.

Notes

1 Howard, 181f. Autograph in Pierpoint Morgan Library, New York.
2 Howard, 195.
3 Cited in *DJ*, 616.
4 *CL* (May 1771), 9:329.
5 *CL* 9:314f. Regarding Arnaud's election to the Académie Française, see Kaplan, 100, 131.
6 *JL* (1781), 4:163–176. *QGP*, 2:541f.
7 *QGP*, 2:544.
8 Kaplan, 131. My translation.
9 Garat, 255f.
10 Garat, 257f. References are to Nicolas Boileau-Despréaux (1636–1711), poet, satirist, and critic and Clément Marot (1496–1544), Protestant poet and author of the *Épigrammes*.
11 Cited from Mme (Amélie) Suard, *Essais de Mémoires sur M. Suard* (Paris, 1820), 129f. by Desnoires, 198f.

12 Kaplan, 145.
13 Asow, 170.
14 Geoffroy, 6:295f.
15 Ibid., 5:154f.
16 Adapted from Howard, 117f.
17 *CS*, 10:122f. Cited by Kaplan, 124.
18 Ginguené, 45f.
19 Reichardt, 671.
20 Howard, 212.

Timeline of major events

Oct 1772	Du Roullet's letter in the *Mercure de France* (*MF*) offers a Gluck opera to the Paris Opéra and criticizes the unnamed Rousseau's attack on French music.
Feb 1773	Letter in the *MF* signed by Gluck offers the opera but now flatters Rousseau.
19 Jun 1773	Official approval granted for Laborde's journey to Italy to negotiate with Piccinni.
Apr 1774	The Gluck/Du Roullet *Iphigénie en Aulide* opens at the Paris Opéra.
May 1774	Period of mourning for the king interrupts Gluck's opera and the final negotiations with Piccinni.
1774–1777	Gluck's four operas hold a near-monopoly at the Paris Opéra.
Dec 1776	Piccinni arrives in Paris and works on *Roland* with Marmontel during 1777.
1776–1778	Arnaud solicits support against Italian music from Martini in Bologna without success but publishes highly embellished versions of Martini's remarks.
1 Jan 1777	*Journal de Paris* (*JP*) founded.
21 Jan 1777	Unprovoked attacks ridiculing Marmontel begin in the *JP*.
23 Jan 1777	*JP* shut down by moral censor.
29 Jan 1777	*JP* resumes publication.
Early 1777	Inflammatory letter signed by Gluck in *L'Année littéraire* ignites the quarrel.
3 Mar 1777	A balanced review of Gluck's *Iphigénie en Aulide* appears in La Harpe's journal.
5 Mar 1777	In the *JP*, the *Anonyme de Vaugirard* (Suard) begins a series of misrepresentations and ridicule of the review in La Harpe's journal.
25 Mar 1777	La Harpe responds once only.
Spring 1777	Marmontel publishes his *Essai sur les révolutions de la musique, en France*, a work of serious criticism.

130 Timeline of major events

1 Jun 1777	In a long series of anonymous letters and epigrams, the *JP* repeatedly ridicules and misrepresents Marmontel's *Essai*. He remains silent.
Aug 1777	La Harpe's journal reviews Marmontel's *Essai* favourably.
15 Aug 1777	In a lead article, the *JP* reviews a pamphlet that insinuates the capital crime of sodomy against La Harpe and David Hume by recalling false accusations against Hume in 1766 by Jean-Jacques Rousseau.
27 Sep 1777	Premiere of Gluck's *Armide* at the Paris Opéra.
5 Oct 1777	La Harpe's journal publishes a balanced critique of Gluck's *Armide*.
12 Oct 1777	In response to La Harpe's review, the *JP* publishes a letter of misrepresentation and sarcasm signed by Gluck.
14 Oct 1777	Many anonymous attacks on La Harpe begin in the *JP*, including several from the *Anonyme*.
21 Oct 1777	The *JP* publishes another letter signed by Gluck, appealing for help from the *Anonyme*.
5 Nov 1777	La Harpe's brief response to attacks marks his exit from the quarrel.
27 Jan 1778	The first performance of *Roland* by Piccinni/Marmontel succeeds beyond expectations.
Feb 1778	The *JP* publishes a letter in support of Piccinni from the Mélophile, incorrectly identified much later as Ginguené.
Feb 1778	Suard takes a long leave of absence. The known *JP* coverage of *querelle*-related material decreases in 1778 and 1779.
May/Jun 1778	Suard gains new influence at the *MF* via Panckoucke's (his brother-in-law) purchase of the *privilège*. The *JP*'s repeated attacks on various subjects in La Harpe's journal lead to its termination. He becomes editor of a new political section in the *MF*.
Jul 1778	Marmontel reviews Prince Beloselskii's *De la musique en Italie* in the *MF*.
15 Aug 1778	Writing anonymously in the *MF*, Suard adds fabrications to Martini's limited praise of Gluck (solicited in 1776 by Arnaud). Suard also rebukes Beloselskii and Marmontel with misrepresentations.
15 Sep 1778	In the *MF*, Marmontel opposes anonymous writing and calls for tolerance. Suard responds anonymously once again on 5 October.
18 May 1779	The Gluck/Guillard *Iphigénie en Tauride* opens at the Paris Opéra.
Jul 1779	After Coquéau independently publishes his *Entretiens* with material favourable to the Piccinnists, the *JP* renews its attacks.
24 Sep 1779	Premiere of the Gluck/Tschudi *Echo et Narcisse* at the Paris Opéra is unsuccessful because the *JP* did not offer its customary support. Gluck leaves Paris and does not return.
22 Feb 1780	Premiere of the Piccinni/Marmontel *Atys* at the Paris Opéra.

	Timeline of major events 131
23 Jan 1781	Premiere of the Piccinni/Dubreuil *Iphigenie en Tauride* at the Paris Opéra.
1781	Publication of *Mémoires pour servir à l'histoire de la révolution opérée dans la musique par M. le chevalier Gluck*, almost entirely a reprint of Gluckist writings.
Feb 1783	Writing anonymously in the *MF*, Suard renews the issues of the *querelle*.
1783	The Mélophile responds in a 27-page pamphlet that is said to have terminated the quarrel.
1784	Arnaud dies.
1784	Piccinni heads vocal instruction at the new Ecole Royale de Musique et de Déclamation.

Index

Alembert, Jean Le Rond d' 6, 59, 72, 74
Algarotti, Francesco 54, 61, 80
Anfossi, Pasquale 104
Angermüller, Rudolph 36
Ariosto, Lodovico 38
Arnaud, François 4, 7–10, 22, 24–35, 37–38, 50, 54, 56–57, 59, 71, 77, 81–82, 84, 86–87, 90, 101, 107, 118–23, 129–31
Arnold, R. J. 61
Arnould, Sophie 19
Asow, Hedwig and E. H. Mueller von 22, 36, 60, 108, 128

Barbier, A. E. 10
Beaumesnil, Henriette Adêlaïde Villard de 69
Beauveau, Charles de, Maréchal de France 50
Beloselskii, Aleksandr 29–30, 33–35, 130
Bemetzrieder, Anton 53
Benda, Georg 110
Berlioz, Hector 20–21, 23, 82, 90
Berton, Pierre 125
Bertoni, Ferdinando Giuseppe 30, 114
Boileau-Despréaux, Nicolas 96, 121
Bonocini, Giovanni Maria 26
Boyer, Pascal 23, 52, 79
Braque, Georges 1
Braunbehrens, Volkmar 117
Buffon, Georges-Louis Leclerc, Comte de 72
Buranelli (probably Buranello, a nickname for B. Galuppi) 30
Burney, Charles 5, 22, 51, 61

Calzabigi, Ranieri 80
Carraccioli, Domenico 12, 14, 28–29, 32, 39, 118
Chabanon, Michel-Paul-Guy de 52
Charlton, David 23
Chastellux (Châtellux), François-Jean, Marquis de 59
Cimarosa, Domenico 113
Clairon, La (Clair-Josèphe-Hippolyte Leris) 72
Colbran, Isabella 114
Condorcet, Nicolas, Marquis de 59, 84, 90
Coquéau, Claude-Philbert 99–100, 107, 130
Corancez, Guillaume Olivier de 3, 14
Corneille, Thomas 34, 96
Cramer, Carl Friedrich 12
Crébillon, Prosper Jolyot de 96

Darlow, Mark 2, 22
Darnton, Robert 22
Davenport, Richard 75–76
Desfontaines, Pierre-François 72
Desnoiresterres, Gustave 22, 50, 60, 90, 127
Devismes, Anne-Pierre-Jacques 55, 104–5, 118
Diderot, Denis 53, 58–59, 61, 72, 119
Dorat, Claude-Joseph 71
Du Barry, Jeanne Bécu 14, 23
Dubreuil, Alphonse du Congé 105, 131
Duclos, Charles Pinot 72
Duni, Egidio Romualdo 44

Du Roullet, François-Louis Le Bland 4–5, 11–13, 39–41, 44, 48, 54, 56–57, 60, 82, 107, 109–12, 126, 129

Epinay, Louise d' 12, 16
Escherny, François-Louis, comte d' 19, 23, 112–15, 117–18

Farinelli (Carlo Broschi) 27, 113
Fénelon, François 69
Fétis, François-Joseph 10, 22
Floquet, Étienne-Joseph 106
Foignet, Charles-Gabriel 84
Folingo, Teofilo 38
Forkel, Johann Nicolaus 109–12, 117
Fortunati, Gian Francesco Maria 32
Fréron, Élie 41
Fréron, Louis-Marie Stanislas 71
Fries, Anna von 112, 118
Fries, Johann von 112

Galiani, Ferdinando 12–13, 22, 61, 70, 103–4
Galuppi, Baldassare 44, 45, 80, 104
Garat, Dominique-Joseph 102, 107, 119, 121–22, 127
Geoffroy, Julien-Louis 116–17, 122–23, 128
Ginguené, Pierre-Louis 13, 17–18, 21–22, 40, 60, 91–96, 98, 104–8, 114–15, 117, 125, 128, 130
Gluck, Christoph Willibald 1–5, 8–22, 62–63, 71, 77, *passim* in 24–59, 79–130
Gossec, François-Joseph 17, 127
Grassini, Josephina 114
Graun, Carl Heinrich 111
Grétry, André-Ernest-Modeste 17, 44, 45, 48, 54, 55
Grimm, Friedrich Melchior von 5, 52, 58–59
Grosier, Jean-Baptiste 71
Guadagni, Gaetano 114
Guillard, Nicolas-François 104, 123, 130
Guy, Pierre 75

Handel, George Frideric 27, 110
Hasse, Faustina Bordoni 114
Hasse, Johann Adolph 27, 45, 111, 113
Heartz, Daniel 61

Helvétius, Claude-Adrien 72
Hénault, Charles-Jean-François 72
Holbach, Paul-Henri Thiry, Baron d' 73–74
Howard, Patricia 22, 60, 108, 127–28
Hume, David 71–76, 130

Isherwood, Robert M. 22, 90

Jerold, Beverly 23, 60, 61
Jommelli, Niccolò 29, 30, 42, 44, 45, 80, 104

Kaplan, James M. 4, 22, 36, 48, 60, 78, 90, 107, 128
Kruthoffer, Franz 104–5, 118

Laborde, Jean-Benjamin de 12–14, 97–98, 107, 114, 117, 129
La Fontaine, Jean de 96
La Harpe, Jean-François de 1, 4–7, 10–11, 18, 29, 36–37, 41–43, 50, 59, 61–72, 77–79, 82–91, 95, 98–103, 107–9, 129–30
Landy, Rémy 107
Larrivée, Henri 69, 93–94
Leblond, Gaspard Michel 7, 10, 11, 22, 33, 35, 36, 60, 61, 83, 89–90, 107, 112, 117, 120
Le Gros, Joseph 17, 19–20, 69, 93, 114
Le Pileur d'Apligny 90
Lespinasse, Julie de 74
Lesure, François 10
Levasseur, Rosalie 34, 37, 69, 94, 104
Loewenberg, Alfred 117
Lully, Jean-Baptiste 21, 38, 43, 53, 88–89, 92, 95, 97–98, 102
Luxe, Jean-Jacques de 74

Majo, Giuseppe de 104
Mannlich, Johann Christian von 19, 23, 124
Marcello, Benedetto 26
Marchesi, Luigi 113
Maria Theresa, Empress 32, 112, 115
Marie Antoinette, Queen 11, 14, 55, 103
Marmontel, Jean-François 1, 4–6, 8, 10–11, 15–16, 23, 29, 30, 34–40, 43–52, 55–63, 70, 73–74, 78, 86, 88, 89, 91–103, 108–9, 118–23, 129–31

Marot, Clément 121, 127
Martini, Giovanni Battista 24–36, 122, 126, 129–30
Meister, Jacques-Henri 52, 53, 58–59
Metastasio, Pietro 40, 80
Monsigny, Pierre-Alexandre 17, 44
Montenoy, Charles Palissot de 126
Monza, Carlo 113
Morellet, André 59
Mossner, Ernest Campbell 78
Mozart, Wolfgang Amadeus 3, 22, 38

Nietzsche, Friedrich 10, 107
Noverre, Jean-Georges 69, 113

Paisiello, Giovanni 104, 113
Panckoucke, Charles-Joseph 33, 68, 99, 130
Pergolesi, Giovanni Battista 44, 45
Philidor, François-André Danican 16–17, 44
Piccinni, Niccolò 1–4, 11–15, 17, 29–33, 38–40, 42, 45, 51, 54–57, 59–60, 69, 80, 91–98, 100, 103–106, 109, 118, 122–27, 129–31
Piron, Alexis 71
Porpora, Nicola Antonio 26
Pougin, Arthur 117

Quinault, Philippe 38, 55, 80, 89, 116

Racine, Jean 54, 87, 96, 110
Rameau, Jean-Philippe 16–17, 19, 21, 43, 53, 69, 76, 116
Rasmussen, Dennis C. 78

Reichardt, Johann Friedrich 125, 128
Ricci, Corrado 36, 117
Rousseau, Jean-Baptiste 96
Rousseau, Jean-Jacques 13–14, 22, 70, 72–78, 85, 121, 129–30

Sacchini, Antonio 1, 30, 45, 55, 62, 80, 87, 93, 104
Saint-Lambert, Jean-François de 59, 122
Salieri, Antonio 12, 115–16
Sarti, Giuseppe 113
Scarlatti, Alessandro 26
Schmid, Anton 35
Sedaine, Michel-Jean 87
Suard, Amélie 122, 127
Suard, Jean-Baptiste-Antoine 1, 4–5, 7–9, 11, 22, 33–34, 36, 38, 41–43, 50, 56–59, 61, 74–75, 81–86, 89, 96, 99–102, 107, 118–22, 129–31

Traetta, Tommaso 45, 55, 62, 104
Tschudi, Jean-Baptiste-Louis-Théodore, Baron de 122, 130
Turgot, Anne-Robert-Jacques 5, 15

Vatielli, Francesco 35, 36
Vauthier, G. 108
Verdelin, Marie-Madeleine, Marquise de 73
Vinci, Leonardo 1, 26
Voltaire (François-Marie Arouet) 5–6, 22, 70, 72, 87, 96

Zaretsky, Robert 78

For Product Safety Concerns and Information please contact our EU representative GPSR@taylorandfrancis.com
Taylor & Francis Verlag GmbH, Kaufingerstraße 24, 80331 München, Germany

www.ingramcontent.com/pod-product-compliance
Lightning Source LLC
Chambersburg PA
CBHW070403240426
43661CB00056B/2519